Featured in cover photo:
Suet Pastry Crescents 66
Strawberry Pancakes 33
Cucumber Salad 41
Chicken Paprika with Spatzle 34

Illustrations by Karen Rolnick

Hungarian Cookbook

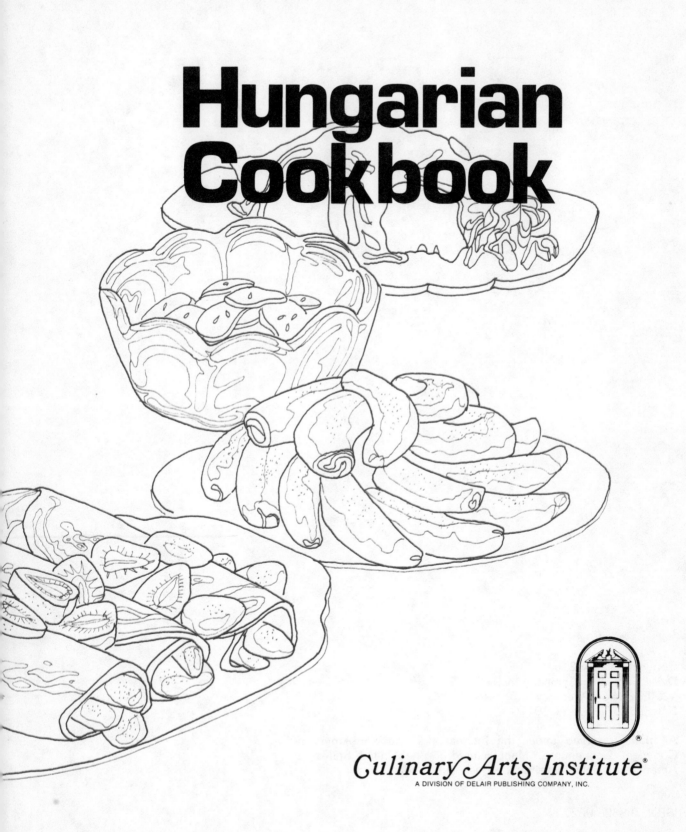

Culinary Arts Institute
A DIVISION OF DELAIR PUBLISHING COMPANY, INC.

ISBN: 0-8326-0627-8

Contents

Hungarian Cookery

The Hungarian daily meal pattern consists of an early but light breakfast, followed by "Tizorai," a more hearty, satisfying breakfast about 10 o'clock. The noon meal is usually the main meal of the day, then a snack in the middle of the afternoon, usually coffee with a piece of rich pastry or coffee cake. The supper is lighter than the noon meal, but on special occasions it may be more elaborate, including appetizers. To accompany their meals, Hungarians customarily drink beer or Tokay, the wine of the country. They also consume large quantities of coffee—plain, diluted with milk or topped with a generous fluffy mound of whipped cream.

The origin of Hungarian foods is not altogether clear. Some foods date back to the days of the Magyar tribes migrating across the Hungarian Plain. Turkish influence is felt by their introduction of paprika—scarcely 100 years ago.

Hungarian main dishes are savory with seasonings—a delicate touch of fiery red, but mildly sweet, paprika or an occasional surprise flavor of dill or caraway seed—and satisfying with the delicious richness that sour cream can lend.

Fascinating recipes are presented in the Hungarian Cookbook—intriguing and rewarding—to lure the adventurous American homemaker into the realm of foreign cookery.

It's Smart to Be Careful

There's No Substitute For Accuracy

Read recipe carefully.

Assemble all ingredients and utensils.

Select pans of proper kind and size. Measure inside, from rim to rim.

Use standard measuring cups and spoons. Use measuring cups with subdivisions marked on sides for liquids. Use graduated nested measuring cups for dry or solid ingredients.

Check liquid measurements at eye level.

Level dry or solid measurements with straightedged knife or spatula.

Sift (before measuring) regular all-purpose flour, or not, in accord with the miller's directions on the package. When using the instant type all-purpose flour, follow package directions and recipes. Level flour in cup with straightedged knife or spatula. Spoon, without sifting, whole-grain types of flour into measuring cup.

Preheat oven at required temperature.

Beat whole eggs until thick and piled softly when recipe calls for well-beaten eggs.

For These Recipes—What To Use

Bread Crumbs—two slices fresh bread equal about 1 cup soft crumbs or cubes. One slice dry or toasted bread equals about ½ cup dry cubes or ¼ cup fine, dry crumbs.

Buttered Crumbs—soft or dry bread or cracker crumbs tossed in melted butter or margarine. Use 1 to 2 tablespoons butter or margarine for 1 cup soft crumbs and 2 to 4 tablespoons butter or margarine for 1 cup dry crumbs.

Cream—light, table or coffee cream containing 18% to 20% butterfat.

Heavy or Whipping Cream—containing not less than 30% butterfat.

Flour—regular all-purpose flour. When substituting for cake flour, use 1 cup minus 2 tablespoons all-purpose flour for 1 cup cake flour.

Grated Peel—whole citrus fruit peel finely grated through colored part only.

Ground Poppy Seeds—freshly ground by grocer using special grinder or ground at home in electric blender. If using electric blender, place into blender container about ½ cup whole poppy seeds at one time. Cover container, turn on motor and grind 3 to 5 min., or until poppy seeds are very finely ground.

½ lb. whole poppy seeds—about 1⅔ cups, whole (about 2½ cups, ground).

Herbs and Spices—ground unless recipe specifies otherwise.

Mushrooms—fresh; use canned if specified in recipe.

Oil—salad, cooking. Use olive oil only when recipe states.

Rotary Beater—hand operated (Dover type) beater, or use electric mixer.

Shortening—a hydrogenated vegetable shortening, all-purpose shortening, butter or margarine. Use lard or oil when specified.

Sugar—granulated (beet or cane).

Vinegar—cider vinegar.

How to Do It

Baste—spoon liquid (or use baster) over cooking food to add moisture and flavor.

Bath (Hot Water)—set a baking pan on oven rack and place the filled baking dish in pan. Surround with very hot water to at least 1-inch depth.

Blanch Almonds—The flavor of almonds is best maintained when almonds are allowed to remain in water the shortest possible time during blanching. Therefore, blanch only about ½ cup at a time; repeat process as many times as necessary for larger amounts.

Bring to rapid boiling enough water to well cover shelled almonds. Drop in almonds. Turn off heat and allow almonds to remain in the water about 1 min.; drain or remove with fork or slotted spoon. Place between folds of absorbent paper; pat dry. Gently squeeze almonds with fingers to remove skins. Place on dry absorbent paper. To dry thoroughly, frequently shift almonds to dry spots on paper.

Toast Nuts—place blanched nuts in a shallow pan. Heat nuts (plain or brushed lightly with cooking oil) in oven at 350°F until delicately browned. Stir and turn occasionally. Or add blanched nuts to a heavy skillet in which butter or margarine (about 1 tablespoon per cup of nuts) has been melted; or use oil. Brown nuts lightly, stirring constantly, over moderate heat.

Boil—cook in liquid in which bubbles rise continually and break on the surface. Boiling temperature of water at sea level is 212°F.

Clean Celery—trim roots and cut off leaves. Leaves may be used for added flavor in soups and stuffings; inner leaves may be left on stalk when serving as relish. Separate stalks, remove blemishes and wash. Proceed as directed in recipe.

Clean Garlic—separate into cloves and remove outer (thin, papery) skin.

Clean Green Pepper—rinse and slice away from pod and stem; trim off any white membrane; rinse away seeds; cut into strips, dice or prepare as directed in recipe.

Clean and Slice Mushrooms—wipe with a clean, damp cloth and cut off tips of stems; slice lengthwise through stems and caps.

Clean Onions (Dry)—cut off root end and a thin slice from stem end; peel and rinse. Prepare as directed in recipe.

Dice—cut into small cubes.

Fold—use flexible spatula and slip it down side of bowl to bottom. Turn bowl quarter turn. Lift spatula through mixture along side of bowl with blade parallel to surface. Turn spatula over to fold lifted mixture across material on surface. Cut down and under; turn bowl and repeat process until material seems blended. With every fourth stroke, bring spatula up through center.

Grate Nuts or Chocolate—use a rotary type grater with hand-operated crank. Follow manufacturer's directions. Grated nuts or chocolate should be fine and light; do not use an electric blender for grating or grinding nuts called for in these recipes.

Grind Nuts—put nuts through medium blade of food chopper.

Hard-Cook Eggs—put eggs into large sauce pan and cover completely with cold or lukewarm water. Cover. Bring water rapidly just to boiling. Turn off heat. If necessary to prevent further boiling, remove pan from heat source. Let stand covered 20 to 22 min. Plunge eggs promptly into running cold water. Roll egg between hands to loosen shell. When cooled, start peeling at large end.

Note: Eggs are a protein food and therefore should never be boiled.

Marinate—allow food to stand in liquid (usually an oil and acid mixture) to impart additional flavor.

Measure Brown Sugar—pack firmly into measuring cup so that sugar will hold shape of cup when turned out.

Measure Granulated Brown Sugar—see substitution table on package before pouring into measuring cup.

Melt Chocolate—unsweetened, over simmering water; sweet or semi-sweet, over hot (not simmering) water.

Mince—cut or chop into small, fine pieces.

Panbroil Bacon—place into a cold skillet only as many bacon slices as will lie flat. Cook slowly, turning frequently. Pour off fat as it collects. When bacon is evenly crisped and browned, remove from skillet and drain on absorbent paper.

Prepare Quick Chicken Broth—dissolve 1 chicken bouillon cube in 1 cup hot water.

Prepare Quick Meat Broth—dissolve 1 meat bouillon cube or ½ teaspoon concentrated meat extract in 1 cup hot water.

Rice—force through ricer, sieve or food mill.

Scald Milk—heat in top of double boiler over simmering water or in a heavy saucepan over direct heat just until a thin film appears.

Sieve—force through coarse sieve or food mill.

Simmer—cook in a liquid just below boiling point; bubbles form slowly and break below surface.

Oven Temperatures
Very Slow...................250°F to 275°F
Slow........................300°F to 325°F
Moderate....................350°F to 375°F
Hot.........................400°F to 425°F
Very Hot....................450°F to 475°F
Extremely Hot...............500°F to 525°F
Use a portable oven thermometer to double-check oven temperture.

When You Deep Fry
About 20 min. before ready to deep fry, fill a deep saucepan one-half to two-thirds full with hydrogenated vegetable shortening, all-purpose shortening, lard or cooking oil for deep frying. Heat fat slowly to temperature given in recipe. A deep-frying thermometer is an accurate guide for deep-frying temperatures.

If thermometer is not available, the following bread cube method may be used as a guide. A 1-in. cube of bread browns in about 60 seconds at 350°F to 375°F.

When using automatic deep fryer, follow manufacturer's directions for amount of fat and timing.

When You Cook Candy or Syrup
A candy thermometer is an accurate guide to correct stage of cooking. Put the thermometer into syrup mixture after sugar is dissolved and boiling starts. A 3-inch depth of syrup is advisable to take an accurate thermometer reading; if necessary, tip pan to obtain depth. If thermometer is cold, heat it in warm water before plunging it into hot syrup.

A Check-List for Successful Baking

✔**Read Again** "It's Smart to Be Careful—There's No Substitute for Accuracy".

✔**Place Oven Rack** so top of product will be almost center of oven. Stagger pans so no pan is directly over another and they do not touch each other or walls of oven. Arrange single pan so that center of product is as near center of oven as possible.

✔**Prepare Pan**—For torte recipe that states "prepare pan," grease bottom of pan only; line with waxed paper cut to fit bottom; grease waxed paper. For most yeast doughs, grease inside of pan. For cookies, lightly grease cookie sheets. If recipe states "set out pan" do not grease or line pan.

✔**Sift** (before measuring) regular all-purpose flour, or not, in accord with the miller's directions on the package. When using the instant type all-purpose flour, follow package directions and recipes. Level flour in cup with straight-edged knife or spatula. Spoon, without sifting, whole-grain types of flour into measuring cup.

✔**Have All Ingredients** at room temperature unless recipe specifies otherwise.

Cream Shortening(alone or with flavorings) by stirring, rubbing or beating with spoon or electric mixer until softened. Add sugar in small amounts, creaming thoroughly after each addition. Thorough creaming helps to insure a fine-grained cake.

✔**Beat Whole Eggs** until thick and piled softly when recipe calls for well-beaten eggs.

✔**Beat Egg Whites** as follows:**Frothy**—entire mass forms bubbles;**Rounded peaks**—peaks turn over slightly when beater is slowly lifted upright; **Stiff peaks**—peaks remain standing when beater is slowly lifted upright.

✔**Beat Egg Yolks** until thick and lemon colored when recipe calls for well-beaten egg yolks.

✔**Apply Baking Tests** when minimum baking time is up. For torte,touch lightly at center; if it springs back, torte is done. Or, insert a cake tester or wooden pick at center; if it comes out clean, torte is done.

✔**Cool Tortes** 15 min. in pans on cooling racks after removing from oven; or cool as recipe states.

✔**Remove Torte** from pan after cooling. Run spatula gently around sides of pan. Cover with cooling rack. Invert and remove pan. Turn right-side up immediately after peeling off waxed paper.Or remove from pan as recipe states. Cool torte completely before frosting.

✔**Fill Tortes**—Spread frosting or filling over top of bottom layer. Repeat procedure if more layers are used. If necessary, hold layers in position with wooden picks; remove when frosting is set.

✔**Frost Filled Tortes**—Frost sides first, working rapidly. See that frosting touches plate all around bottom, leaving no gaps. Pile remaining frosting on top of torte and spread lightly.

✔**Test** for lukewarm liquid (80°F to 85°F) by placing a drop on wrist; it will feel neither hot nor cold.

✔**Knead Dough** by folding opposite side over toward you. Using heel of hands, gently push dough away. Give it a quarter turn. Repeat process rhythmically until dough is smooth and elastic, 5 to 8 min., using as little additional flour as possible. Always turn the dough in the same direction.

✔**Remove Rolls, Bread and Cookies** from pans as they come from oven, unless otherwise directed. Set on cooling racks.

How to Cook Vegetables

Wash fresh vegetables, but do not soak them in water for any length of time.If they are wilted, put them in cold water for a few minutes. Cauliflower, broccoli, artichokes and Brussels sprouts may be immersed in cold salted water a few minutes before they are cooked.

Baking—Bake such vegetables as potatoes, tomatoes and squash without removing skins. Pare vegetables for oven dishes, following directions given with recipes.

Boiling—Have water boiling rapidly before adding vegetables. Add salt at beginning of cooking period (¼ teaspoon per cup of water). After adding vegetables, again bring water to boiling as quickly as possible. If more water is needed, add boiling water. Boil at a moderate rate and cook vegetables until just tender.

In general, cook vegetables in a covered pan in the smallest amount of water as possible and in the shortest possible time. Exceptions for amounts of water for covering are:

Asparagus—arrange in tied bundles with stalks standing in bottom of double boiler containing water to cover lower half of spears—cover with inverted double boiler top.

Broccoli—trimmed of leaves and bottoms of stalks. If stalks are over 1 in. in diameter, make lengthwise gashes through them almost to flowerets. Cook quickly in a covered skillet or saucepan in 1 in. of boiling, salted water 10 to 15 min., or just until tender.

Cabbage (mature)—cooked, loosely covered, in just enough water to cover. Cabbage (young) cooked, tightly covered, in a minimum amount of water (do not overcook).

To restore color to red cabbage, add small amount of vinegar at end of cooking time.

Caulifower (whole head) —cooked, uncovered, in a 1 in. depth of boiling, salted water for 5 min. then covered, 15 to 20 min.

Mature Root Vegetables (potatoes, rutabagas, parsnips)— cooked, covered, in just enough boiling, salted water to cover vegetables.

Spinach—cooked, covered, with only the water which clings to leaves after final washing.

Broiling—Follow directions with specific recipes.

Panning—Finely shred or slice vegetables. Cook slowly until just tender in a small amount of fat, in a covered, heavy pan. Occasionally move with spoon to prevent sticking and burning.

Steaming—Cooking in a pressure saucepan is a form of steaming. Follow directions given with saucepan because overcooking may occur in a matter of seconds.

Note: Some saucepans having tight-fitting covers may lend themselves to steaming vegetables in as little as 1 teaspoon water, no water or a small amount of butter, margarine or shortening.

Canned Vegetables—Reduce liquid from can to one-half of the original amount by boiling rapidly. Add vegetables and heat thoroughly.

Home-Canned Vegetables—Boil 10 min. (not required for tomatoes and sauerkraut).

Dried (Dehydrated) Vegetables—Soak and cook as directed in specific recipes.

Frozen Vegetables—Do not thaw before cooking (thaw corn on cob and partially thaw spinach). Break frozen block apart with fork during cooking. Use as little boiling salted water as possible for cooking. Follow directions on package.

Appetizers

Chopped Chicken Livers

2   **hard-cooked eggs**
1   **lb. chicken livers**
2   **tablespoons chicken fat or butter**
1   **small onion**
4   **sprigs parsley**
¼   **cup cream**
1   **teaspoon salt**
½   **teaspoon dry mustard**
½   **teaspoon paprika**
¼   **teaspoon nutmeg or marjoram**
⅛   **teaspoon freshly ground pepper**

1. Set out a heavy 10-in. skillet and a wooden bowl or cutting board.
2. Prepare eggs and set aside.
3. Meanwhile, rinse chicken livers with cold water and drain on absorbent paper.
4. Melt chicken fat or butter in the skillet over low heat.
5. Add livers; turning occasionally, cook 5 to 10 min., or until lightly browned. Remove from heat and set aside until livers are cool.
6. Remove livers with slotted spoon to bowl or cutting board; reserve drippings. Finely chop chicken livers, eggs, onion, and parsley.
7. Blend ingredients together in a bowl and set aside.
8. Combine the reserved drippings and cream
9. Blend in a mixture of salt, mustard, paprika, nutmeg or marjoram, and pepper.
10. Combine with liver mixture, mixing thoroughly. Chill in refrigerator for about 4 hrs. to allow flavors to blend.
11. Garnish servings with sprigs of parsley. (Allow about ¼ cup of Chopped Chicken Livers per serving.) Serve with crisp, dry toast.

10 to 12 servings

Cream Cheese "Liptauer" Spread

1	pkg. (8 oz.) cream cheese
½	cup butter or margarine
3	tablespoons thick sour cream
2	anchovy fillets
1	teaspoon capers
1	tablespoon finely chopped onion or chives
1	tablespoon prepared mustard
1½	teaspoons paprika
1	teaspoon caraway seeds
½	teaspoon salt
	Paprika
10	stuffed and rolled anchovy fillets

1. Cream together cream cheese, butter or margarine, and sour cream in a bowl until well blended.
2. Mash 2 anchovy fillets and capers together with mortar and pestle or with fork and add to cheese mixture.
3. Add onion or chives, mustard, paprika, caraway seeds and salt to cheese mixture and blend ingredients thoroughly.
4. Transfer mixture to a serving plate and shape into a smooth mound. Make slight indentations in mound with tines of a fork. Sprinkle with paprika.
5. Insert wooden picks into 10 anchovy fillets.
6. Place on mound. Chill slightly in refrigerator.
7. Garnish by arranging parsley sprigs around mound. Serve with crackers, pumpernickel or rye bread.

1¾ cups spread

Cottage Cheese "Liptauer" Spread: Follow recipe for Cream Cheese "Liptauer" Spread. Substitute 1 cup (about ½ lb.) **cream-style cottage cheese,** drained, for cream cheese. Press cottage cheese through a ricer or fine sieve.

Ham-Stuffed Eggs

6	hard-cooked eggs
⅓	cup very finely chopped cooked ham
¾	teaspoon dry mustard
½	teaspoon salt
¼	teaspoon pepper
4	tablespoons thick sour cream
1	tablespoon butter, melted
	Paprika

1. Prepare eggs.
2. Cut each egg into halves lengthwise. Remove egg yolks to a bowl and mash them with a fork or press through ricer or sieve into a bowl. Set egg whites aside. Mix egg yolks with cooked ham and a mixture of mustard, salt and pepper.
3. Stir in sour cream, moistening to a thick, paste-like consistency.
4. Fill the egg whites with egg yolk mixture, leaving tops rounded and rough. Serve chilled or hot.
5. To heat, arrange egg halves, filled-side up, in a buttered 8-in. sq. baking dish. Brush eggs lightly with butter.
6. Sprinkle eggs with paprika.
7. Place in 375°F oven about 5 min., or until heated thoroughly.
8. To serve, cut egg halves into smaller pieces and insert a wooden pick into each.

6 to 8 servings

Anchovy-Stuffed Eggs: Follow recipe for Ham-Stuffed Eggs. Substitute 4 or 5 **anchovy fillets.** very finely chopped, for the ham and omit salt.

Mushroom-Stuffed Eggs: Follow recipe for Ham-Stuffed Eggs. Omit the ham and decrease sour cream to 2 to 3 tablespoons. Clean and very finely chop ¼ lb. **mushrooms.** Cook slowly in a small skillet in 2 to 3 tablespoons **butter or margarine,** stirring gently until lightly browned and tender. Stir into egg yolk mixture.

Soups & Accompaniments

Cherry Soup

1	qt. water
2½	lbs. sweetened frozen tart cherries, slightly thawed
½	teaspoon salt
½	cup cold water
¼	cup all-purpose flour
3	egg yolks, slightly beaten
1	cup thick sour cream

1. Bring 1 qt. water to boiling in a 3-qt. saucepan having a tight-fitting cover.
2. Add cherries and salt to the water, breaking frozen blocks apart with fork.
3. Bring to boiling again. Cover saucepan and simmer cherries 10 min.
4. Meanwhile, put ½ cup cold water into a 1-pt. screw-top jar.
5. Sprinkle flour onto it.
6. Cover jar tightly; shake until ingredients are well blended. Slowly pour flour-water mixture into cherry mixture, stirring constantly. Bring again to boiling. Cook 3 to 5 min., stirring occasionally. Remove from heat. Vigorously stir about ⅓ cup hot soup gradually into egg yolks.
7. Immediately blend into hot soup. Stirring constantly, cook over low heat 2 to 3 min. (Do not overcook or allow soup to boil.) Remove immediately from heat. Gradually add, stirring vigorously, about 1 cup hot soup to sour cream.
8. Immediately blend into remaining soup. Cool slightly. Place in refrigerator to chill.

About 6 servings

Note: Fresh sour red cherries, pitted, can be substituted for the frozen cherries. Sweeten the soup to taste.

Cherry Soup with Sweet Cream: Follow recipe for Cherry Soup. Cook a 1-in. piece **stick cinnamon** with cherries; remove and discard cinnamon before adding the flour-water mixture. Substitute **light or heavy cream** for sour cream; add directly to soup, stirring constantly.

Cherry Soup with Wine: Follow recipe for Cherry Soup. Decrease boiling water to 3½ cups. Before chilling soup, stir in ½ cup **sherry.**

Mushroom Soup

1	veal soup bone, cracked
1½	qts. water
1½	teaspoons salt
4	sprigs parsley
3	peppercorns
4	medium-size carrots (about 1 cup, sliced)
1	lb. mushrooms
½	cup butter or margarine
1	small onion, chopped
2	tablespoons chopped parsley
1	teaspoon paprika
½	teaspoon salt
	Croutons (1½ times recipe, page 16)
4	egg yolks, slightly beaten
1	cup thick sour cream
1	teaspoon lemon juice

1. Set out a large kettle or sauce pot having a tight-fitting cover and a heavy 10-in. skillet having a tight-fitting cover.
2. Have veal soup bone ready.
3. Put soup bone into kettle with water, 1½ teaspoon salt, 4 sprigs parsley, and peppercorns.
4. Bring water to boiling. Skim off and discard foam. Cover kettle and simmer soup about 1 hr., skimming as necessary.
5. Shortly before end of cooking period, cut off and discard tops, wash, pare or scrape and cut carrots into ¼-in. slices.
6. Add carrots to kettle, cover and simmer 15 to 20 min., or until carrots are tender.
7. Meanwhile, clean and slice mushrooms.
8. Melt butter or margarine in the skillet.
9. Add mushrooms with onion, 2 tablespoons chopped parsley, paprika and ½ teaspoon salt.
10. Cook slowly, stirring gently, 5 to 8 min., or until mushrooms and onions are lightly browned and tender; set aside.
11. Prepare croutons and set aside.
12. Remove kettle from heat. Remove and discard bone, peppercorns and parsley sprigs. Blend contents of skillet into soup. Vigorously stir ⅓ cup of the hot soup gradually into egg yolks.
13. Immediately blend into hot soup. Stirring constantly, cook over low heat 2 to 3 min. (Do not overcook or allow soup to boil.) Remove immediately from heat and cover.
14. Combine sour cream and lemon juice in a bowl.
15. Add gradually, stirring vigorously, about 1 cup hot soup to sour cream mixture. Immediately blend into remaining hot soup. Heat thoroughly, but do not boil. Serve with the croutons.

6 or 7 servings

Sweet Cream Mushroom Soup: Follow recipe for Mushroom Soup. Substitute 1 cup **heavy or light cream** for the thick sour cream, adding it directly to the soup. Omit the lemon juice.

Beef Barley Soup

2	quarts water
1	soup bone with meat
½	cup chopped celery tops
1	tablespoon salt
½	teaspoon pepper
½	cup uncooked regular barley
3	cups coarsely chopped cabbage
1	cup sliced carrots
1	cup sliced celery
2	cups sliced parsnips
2	cups thinly sliced onion
1	can (12 ounces) tomato paste

1. Combine water, bone, celery tops, salt, and pepper in a Dutch oven. Bring to boiling; cover tightly and simmer 1 to 2 hours.
2. Remove bone from stock; cool. Remove meat from bone; chop. Return to stock.
3. Stir in barley; continue cooking 30 minutes.
4. Add remaining ingredients; simmer 30 minutes, or until vegetables are tender.

8 to 10 servings

Beef Broth

1½	lbs. lean beef (boneless chuck or plate)
1	beef soup bone, cracked
1	veal soup bone, cracked
2	qts. water
1	tablespoon salt
8	peppercorns
4	medium-size carrots, washed and scraped or pared
3	medium-size (about 1 lb.) potatoes, washed and pared
1	large onion
1	medium-size green pepper
¼	small head (about ½ lb.) cabbage, rinsed
3	12 in. stalks celery (including leaves), cut in pieces
10	sprigs parsley
	Hot water (enough to cover vegetables)

1. Set out a large kettle having a tight-fitting cover.
2. Have beef, beef soup bone, and veal soup bone ready.
3. Put meat and soup bones into kettle with water, salt and peppercorns.
4. Bring water to boiling. Reduce heat immediately. Cover kettle and simmer 2 hrs., skimming off and discarding foam as necessary.
5. Then add carrots, potatoes, onion, pepper, cabbage, celery and parsley to broth.
6. Pour hot water into kettle.
7. Cover kettle and simmer 2 hrs. longer, or until meat is tender when pierced with a fork. Remove meat and vegetables with slotted spoon to a serving platter. Cover platter and keep them warm. Remove and discard soup bones. Strain the broth through fine sieve into tureen; discard peppercorns.
8. Cut meat into serving-size pieces and serve with vegetables after serving the broth.
9. If desired. serve the broth with **Liver Dumplings** (page 17) or **Noodles** (page 17).

6 to 8 servings

Croutons

3	tablespoons butter or margarine
2	slices toasted bread

1. Melt butter or margarine over low heat in a large, heavy skillet.
2. Meanwhile, if desired, trim crusts from bread.
3. Cut bread into ¼- to ½-in. cubes. Put into skillet and stir until all sides are coated; remove from heat.

About 1¼ cups Croutons

Caraway Soup

⅓	cup butter
⅓	cup all-purpose flour
1½	tablespoons caraway seeds
1½	teaspoons salt
⅛	teaspoon freshly ground pepper
¾	teaspoon paprika
1½	qts. water
	Croutons (1½ times recipe, page 16)
2	egg yolks, slightly beaten

1. Melt butter over low heat in a 2-qt. saucepan having a tight-fitting cover.
2. Blend in a mixture of flour, caraway seeds, salt and pepper.
3. Heat until mixture bubbles and is lightly browned, stirring constantly. Remove from heat. Blend in paprika.
4. Add water gradually, stirring constantly.
5. Return to heat and bring rapidly to boiling stirring constantly. Cover and simmer 15 min.
6. Meanwhile, prepare croutons and set aside.
7. Remove soup from heat. Vigorously stir about 3 tablespoons of the hot soup into egg yolks.
8. Immediately blend into hot soup. Stirring constantly, cook over low heat 2 to 3 min. (Do not overcook or allow soup to boil.) Remove soup from heat at once. Pour through sieve; discard caraway seeds. Serve with croutons.

About 6 servings

Creamed Caraway Soup: Follow recipe for Caraway Soup. Just before serving, blend into soup ¾ cup **heavy cream.**

Liver Dumplings

Beef Broth (page 16)
1   **cup fine cracker crumbs**
¾   **cup milk**
½   **lb. liver (beef, lamb, veal or calf's), sliced ¼ to ½ in. thick**
1   **tablespoon fat**
1   **small onion, quartered**
½   **cup sifted all-purpose flour**
1   **teaspoon chopped parsley**
½   **teaspoon salt**
¼   **teaspoon marjoram**
⅛   **teaspoon pepper**
1   **egg, well beaten**

1. Set out an 8-in. skillet.
2. Prepare Beef Broth.
3. About one-half hour before meat in broth is tender, mix cracker crumbs and milk together in a small bowl and set aside.
4. Cut away, if necessary, tubes and outer membrane from liver.
5. Heat fat in the skillet.
6. Add liver and brown on both sides over medium heat. Cool liver slightly. Put liver through medium blade of food chopper with onion.
7. Using a fork, blend liver into a mixture of flour, chopped parsley, salt, marjoram and pepper.
8. Set aside.
9. Mix cracker mixture with egg.
10. Make a well in liver mixture; add egg mixture all at one time. Stir with a fork until evenly blended. Set aside.
11. After removing meat, vegetables and soup bones from the broth, bring the broth to boiling. Drop dumpling batter by rounded teaspoonfuls into broth. (Batter will drop more readily from a moist spoon.) Cook only one layer of dumplings at one time; do not crowd. Cover tightly and cook 3 to 5 min., or until dumplings rise to surface of broth. Remove dumplings with slotted spoon to soup tureen or large serving bowl. Strain broth over dumplings.

6 to 8 servings

Noodles

1   **cup sifted all-purpose flour**
½   **teaspoon salt**
1   **egg, slightly beaten**
2   **tablespoons water**
2   **qts. water**
2   **teaspoons salt**

1. Sift together flour and salt into a bowl.
2. Make a well in center of flour mixture and add egg.
3. While blending ingredients, add water gradually.
4. Dough should be stiff. Turn dough out onto a lightly floured surface. Shape dough into a ball and knead. Cover dough and let it rest about 5 min.
5. Roll dough on lightly floured surface to 1/8-in. thickness. If sticking occurs, loosen dough from surface with knife or spatula; sprinkle flour underneath. Turn dough over and continue rolling until paper thin. Allow dough to partially dry about 1 hr.
6. Cut dough into lengthwise strips, 2½-in. wide, and stack on top of each other. Slice into short strips 1/16 to 1/8-in. wide. Separate noodles and allow to dry thoroughly. (Noodles can be stored in a tightly covered container if not cooked immediately.)

About ⅓ lb. Noodles

1. For Cooking Noodles—Bring water and salt to rapid boiling in a 3 or 4-qt. saucepan.
2. Add noodles gradually to water so that boiling will not stop. Boil noodles uncovered, stirring occasionally with a fork, 6 to 10 min., or until soft when pressed against side of pan. Drain in colander or sieve. Rinse with hot water and drain again.

About 2½ cups cooked Noodles

Note: This recipe yields enough noodles for recipes in this cookbook which require them. Double recipe if extra noodles are to be stored for future use.

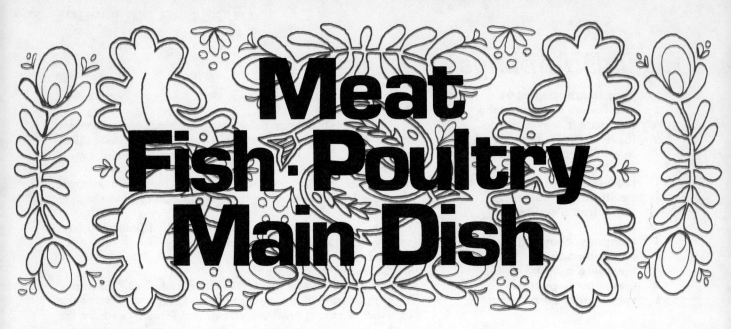

Beef Roll

2	**hard-cooked eggs**
1½	**lbs. round steak, sliced ½ in. thick**
3	**slices bacon, cut in 1-in. pieces**
1	**teaspoon chopped parsley**
½	**teaspoon capers**
½	**teaspoon salt**
⅛	**teaspoon pepper**
3	**tablespoons fat**
1	**teaspoon paprika**
¼	**teaspoon salt**
1	**cup hot water**
3	**tablespoons all-purpose flour**
¼	**teaspoon salt**
⅛	**teaspoon pepper**
1	**cup thick sour cream**

1. Set out a large, heavy skillet having a tight-fitting cover.
2. Prepare hard-cooked eggs, finely chop and set aside.
3. Set out round steak and spread flat on a wooden board or working surface.
4. Cover steak with a mixture of the chopped egg and bacon, chopped parsley, capers, salt and pepper.
5. Roll up steak lengthwise and tie with a cord or fasten with skewers.
6. Heat fat in the skillet.
7. Add steak and slowly brown on all sides.
8. Sprinkle over steak a mixture of paprika and salt.
9. Slowly pour hot water into the skillet.
10. Cover and simmer 1½ to 2 hrs., or until steak is tender when pierced with a fork. Remove from skillet to serving platter; cover platter and keep steak warm.
11. For Gravy—Pour drippings from skillet into a bowl, leaving brown residue in skillet. Allow fat to rise to surface of drippings; skim off and reserve fat. Set aside remaining drippings to be used as part of the liquid; cool to lukewarm. Measure 3 tablespoons reserved fat into the skillet. Blend flour, salt and pepper into fat until smooth.
12. Heat until mixture bubbles. Remove from heat and add liquid (drippings or Quick Meat Broth) gradually, stirring constantly.
13. Return skillet to heat and bring rapidly to boiling, stirring constantly. While stirring, scrape bottom and sides of skillet to blend in brown residue. Cook 1 to 2 min. longer. Remove from heat. Stirring gravy vigorously with a French whip, whisk beater, or fork, add sour cream in very small amounts.
14. Heat thoroughly over low heat, 3 to 5 min., stirring constantly; do not boil.
15. Remove cord or skewers from roll. Slice meat and serve with the gravy.

About 4 servings

Goulash

1½	lbs. boneless pot roast of beef, chuck or blade
2	cups Quick Meat Broth
4	slices bacon
1½	cups (about 3 medium-size) chopped onion
1	tablespoon paprika
1½	teaspoons salt
¼	teaspoon freshly ground pepper
⅛	teaspoon marjoram
¼	cup (about 1 small) chopped green pepper
¾	cup dry white wine
½	cup water
¼	cup all-purpose flour
1	tablespoon butter
½	teaspoon paprika
1	tablespoon water

1. Set out a Dutch oven or a heavy 3-qt. sauce pot having a tight-fitting cover.
2. Set out boneless pot roast of beef, chuck or blade on wooden board and cut into 1½-in. pieces.
3. Prepare Quick Meat Broth and set aside.
4. Dice bacon and place into the sauce pot. Cook slowly, stirring and turning frequently, until bacon is lightly browned. Remove bacon with slotted spoon from sauce pot to small bowl and set aside.
5. Add chopped onion to the bacon fat in the sauce and cook over medium heat until onion is almost tender, stirring occasionally. Remove onion with slotted spoon to bowl containing bacon and set aside.
6. Add meat to the bacon fat and slowly brown on all sides, stirring occasionally. Sprinkle evenly over the meat a mixture of paprika, salt, ground pepper and marjoram.
7. Stir in the bacon-onion mixture with chopped green pepper.
8. Slowly pour in the reserved meat broth and dry white wine.
9. Bring to boiling. Reduce heat, cover sauce pot and simmer 2 to 2½ hrs., or until meat is tender when pierced with a fork. Remove meat with slotted spoon to hot serving dish. Thicken cooking liquid if desired.
10. *To Thicken Cooking Liquid*—Pour water into 1-pt. screw-top jar. Sprinkle flour into the liquid. Cover jar tightly and shake until mixture is well blended. Slowly pour one-half of the mixture into the sauce pot, stirring constantly. Bring to boiling. Gradually add only what is needed of remaining flour-water mixture for consistency desired. Bring to boiling after each addition. After final addition, cook 3 to 5 min. longer.
11. Melt butter in a small skillet. Remove from heat. Blend in paprika. Stir in water. Immediately add to liquid in sauce pot, stirring until well blended. Pour this sauce over meat.
12. Serve immediately.

6 to 8 servings

Goulash with Caraway Seeds: Follow recipe for Goulash. Add 1 teaspoon **caraway seeds** with other seasonings.

Goulash with Garlic: Follow recipe for Goulash. Decrease onion to ¾ cup. Combine onion and green pepper with 1 clove **garlic,** minced.

Goulash with Potatoes: Follow recipe for Goulash. Use 4-qt. sauce pot or kettle. About ½ hr. before end of cooking time, add 6 medium (2 lbs.) **potatoes,** washed, pared and quartered.

Goulash with Tomatoes: Follow recipe for Goulash. Substitute 1 cup (one half 16-oz. can) **tomatoes,** sieved, for one-half of the beef broth.

Goulash with Carrots: Follow recipe for Goulash. About ½ hr. before end of cooking time, add 4 medium size **carrots,** washed, scraped or pared and cut into ½-in. pieces.

Szekely Goulash

1½	lbs. lean leg of pork or pork shoulder
2	tablespoons all-purpose flour
2	teaspoons paprika
1½	teaspoons salt
2	tablespoons fat
2	tablespoons finely chopped onion
3	tablespoons hot water
27	oz. can sauerkraut (about 3½ cups, firmly packed)
2	cups hot water
1½	cups thick sour cream

1. Set out a 4-qt. sauce pot or a Dutch oven having a tight-fitting cover.
2. Put lean leg of pork or pork shoulder onto wooden board and cut into 1½-in. cubes.
3. To coat meat evenly, shake cubes in plastic bag containing a mixture of flour, paprika and salt. Set aside.
4. Cook fat and onion in the sauce pot over medium heat, stirring occasionally, until onion is soft.
5. Add contents of plastic bat to sauce pot; brown meat on all sides, turning occasionally. Add 3 tablespoons water.
6. Cover sauce pot and simmer 1 hr., stirring occasionally; add small amounts of water as needed.
7. Shortly before end of one-hour cooking period, drain contents of can of sauerkraut.
8. If desired, rinse sauerkraut in cold water, so that the goulash will have a milder flavor; drain again. Mix sauerkraut with the meat; add 2 cups hot water.
9. Bring to boiling; cover and simmer ½ hr. longer, or until meat is tender when pierced with a fork. Remove sauce pot from heat. Gradually blend about 1½ cups cooking liquid into sour cream.
10. Blend into hot mixture. Stirring constantly, cook over low heat, 3 to 5 min., until heated thoroughly. Do not boil. Serve in small bowls.

6 to 8 servings

Beef Tongue with Tomato Sauce

4	lbs. fresh beef tongue, rinsed
	Hot water (enough to cover tongue)
1	tablespoon salt
3	bay leaves
1	stalk celery, including leaves, cut in pieces
1	small onion
1	teaspoon peppercorns
1½	cups (2 6-oz. cans) tomato paste
1¼	cups (10½-to 11-oz. can) condensed tomato soup
¾	cup water
½	teaspoon thyme
	Spatzle (see Chicken Paprika with Spatzle, page 34)

1. A heavy 10-in. skillet having a tight-fitting cover will be needed.
2. Place tongue into a 4-qt. kettle or sauce pot having a tight-fitting cover.
3. Add water, salt, bay leaves, celery, onion and peppercorns.
4. Cover kettle and simmer 3 to 4 hrs., or until tongue is tender when pierced with a fork. Place tongue on platter.
When cool enough to handle, remove skin, cut away roots, gristle and small bones at thick end. Diagonally cut tongue into ¼-in. thick slices. Place tongue slices into skillet and set aside.
5. *For Tomato Sauce*—Mix tomato paste, tomato soup, ¾ cup water, and thyme together.
6. Pour the sauce over tongue, cover skillet and simmer about 20 min.
7. Meanwhile prepare Spatzle.
8. Serve tongue and sauce with the noodles.

9 to 12 servings

Sliced Tongue with Anchovy Sauce: Follow recipe for Beef Tongue with Tomato Sauce. Omit tomato sauce. Serve slices of hot tongue with the following anchovy sauce: Place 4 teaspoons **anchovy paste** into a small bowl and gradually add ½ cup **thick sour cream,** stirring constantly. Blend anchovy mixture with 1½ cups **thick sour cream** and ⅓ cup chopped **parsley** in top of double boiler. Heat thoroughly over simmering water, stirring occasionally. Place sauce into serving bowl and garnish with about 2½ tablespoons buttered, fine dry **bread crumbs.**

Stuffed Cabbage

½	**lb. beef short ribs**
½	**teaspoon salt**
	Water to cover
2	**medium-size (about 2 lbs. each) heads cabbage**
	Boiling water
2	**eggs well beaten**
1½	**teaspoons salt**
¼	**teaspoon paprika**
⅛	**teaspoon freshly ground pepper**
1½	**lbs. ground lean pork, such as shoulder**
⅛	**lb. ground smoked pork shoulder butt**
1	**small onion, slivered**
1½	**cloves garlic, minced**
¼	**cup uncooked rice**
1	**27 oz. can sauerkraut (total yield is about 3½ cups firmly packed sauerkraut plus juice)**
1	**cup (8 oz. can) tomato sauce**
	Water (enough to cover contents of kettle)
1	**cup cooking liquid**
2	**tablespoons fat**
2	**tablespoons finely chopped onion**
2	**tablespoons all-purpose flour**
1	**teaspoon paprika**

1. Set out an 8-qt. kettle having a tight-fitting cover.
2. Have ribs ready.
3. Place ribs into the kettle with salt and water.
4. Bring quickly to boiling; skim foam from liquid and discard. Reduce heat; cover and simmer 30 min., skimming as necessary.
5. Meanwhile, remove and discard wilted outer leaves, rinse and cut one-half the core from heads of cabbage.
6. Place cabbage in a large bowl and cover with boiling water.
7. Let stand 1 to 2 min. Take cabbage out of the water; drain. One by one, carefully remove leaves that can be taken off easily; be careful not to tear leaves. Return remainder of cabbage to the water for 1 to 2 min. and repeat process. Remove a total of 18 to 20 leaves. Carefully trim down the thick, heavy part of each leaf. Set leaves aside. Store remainder of cabbage in refrigerator for use in other cooking.
8. Blend together eggs, salt, paprika and pepper.
9. Mix egg mixture lightly and thoroughly with lean pork shoulder butt, onion, garlic and rice.
10. To stuff the cabbage leaves, place on the center of each leaf about ¼ cup of the meat mixture. Roll each leaf tucking the ends in toward center. If desired, use wooden picks to fasten the leaves securely. Set aside.
11. Cover ribs in kettle with one-half contents of sauerkraut.
12. Lay stuffed cabbage carefully on the top of the layer of sauerkraut. Cover stuffed cabbage with remaining sauerkraut. Pour tomato sauce over sauerkraut.
13. Add water.
14. Bring to boiling. Reduce heat; cover and simmer about 2 hrs.
15. Remove stuffed cabbage, sauerkraut and ribs with slotted spoon to a large bowl. Cover to keep warm and set aside. Remove from kettle cooking liquid and set aside to cool to lukewarm.
16. Melt fat in a small skillet.
17. Add onion to fat and cook until almost tender, stirring frequently.
18. Thoroughly blend in a mixture of flour and paprika.
19. Stirring constantly, heat until mixture bubbles. Remove from heat. Gradually add the 1 cup of reserved cooking liquid, stirring constantly until smooth. Blend into liquid in kettle and bring rapidly to boiling; cook 1 or 2 min. longer. Pour sauce over stuffed cabbage. Serve with sauerkraut and ribs.

8 servings

Esterhazy Steak

½   cup all-purpose flour
2   lbs. round steak, cut 1 in. thick
¼   cup all-purpose flour
2   teaspoons salt
½   teaspoon pepper
⅓   cup fat
3   carrots, washed, scraped or pared and thinly sliced
2   small onions thinly sliced
1   parsnip washed, pared and thinly sliced
1   stalk celery, chopped
1   cup Quick Meat Broth
1   teaspoon capers
1   tablespoon fat
1   tablespoon all-purpose flour
¼   teaspoon salt
     Few grains pepper
¼   cup dry white wine
1   cup thick sour cream
1   teaspoon paprika

1. Grease an 11x7x1½-in. baking dish; set out aluminum foil and a large, heavy skillet.
2. Set out flour.
3. Have round steak ready and place on a flat working surface or wooden board.
4. Repeatedly pound meat on one side with meat hammer, pounding in about one-half of the flour. (Pounding increases tenderness.) Turn meat over and repeat process, using remaining flour. Cut meat into serving-size pieces and coat well with a mixture of flour, salt, and pepper.
5. Heat fat in the skillet.
6. Slowly brown meat on both sides. Arrange meat in the baking dish and set aside.
7. Cook carrots, onions, parsnip and celery slowly in the skillet 10 min., stirring occasionally.
8. Meanwhile, prepare quick meat broth and set aside to cool to lukewarm.
9. Spoon the vegetables over the steak. Add capers.
10. Heat fat in the skillet.
11. Blend into fat flour, salt and pepper.
12. Heat until mixture bubbles and is lightly browned, stirring constantly. Remove skillet from heat. Gradually add reserved meat broth, stirring constantly. Return to heat and bring rapidly to boiling, stirring constantly. Remove from heat. Blend in dry white wine.
13. Pour sauce over vegetables and meat in baking dish. Cover dish tightly with aluminum foil.
14. Bake at 350°F 1¼ hrs. Remove aluminum foil; spread over vegetables a mixture of sour cream and paprika.
15. Return dish to oven, uncovered, and continue to bake about 15 min., or until meat is tender when pierced with a fork.

5 or 6 servings

Hot Pickled Beef

4	lbs. boneless pot roast (rump, chuck, blade or round)
	Vinegar
	Water
1	teaspoon salt
10	peppercorns
10	juniper berries
2	bay leaves
1	small onion, coarsely chopped
1	lemon, washed and cut in ¼-in. slices
2	tablespoons butter
	Reserved marinade
	Hot water
¼	cup butter
¼	cup all-purpose flour
3	cups reserved cooking liquid

1. A heavy 4-qt. kettle having a tight-fitting cover will be needed. Set out a deep 3-or 4-qt. bowl having a tight-fitting cover.
2. Have pot roast ready.
3. Place meat into the bowl and cover with a mixture of equal parts of vinegar and water.
4. Add salt, peppercorns, juniper berries, bay leaves, onions and lemon.
5. Cover bowl and put into refrigerator. Marinate meat 2 to 3 days, turning meat once a day.
6. Set out the kettle and cover.
7. Remove meat from marinade and drain thoroughly. Strain and reserve marinade; discard seasonings.
8. Melt butter in the kettle over medium heat.
9. Add meat to butter and brown on both sides. Cover meat with a mixture of equal parts of reserved marinade and water.
10. Bring liquid to boiling. Reduce heat, cover kettle tightly and simmer 3 to 4 hrs. or until meat is tender when pierced with a fork. Remove meat to a warm, deep platter; cover and keep meat warm. Pour off cooking liquid and set aside.
11. For Gravy—Melt butter in the kettle.
12. Throughly blend flour into butter.
13. Heat until mixture bubbles and is lightly browned, stirring constantly. Remove from heat and add 3 cups of reserved cooking liquid gradually, stirring constantly.
14. Return to heat and bring rapidly to boiling stirring constantly; cook 1 to 2 min. longer. Slice meat and pour the gravy over it.
6 to 8 servings

Beef in Lemon Sauce

3	cups cubed, cooked beef
½	cup Quick Meat Broth
4	slices bacon
1	tablespoon fat
1	tablespoon all-purpose flour
1	cup thick sour cream
1	tablespoon lemon juice
1	teaspoon grated lemon peel
½	teaspoon sugar

1. Set out a 10-in. skillet having a tight-fitting cover.
2. Cut beef into ½-in. cubes.
3. Set aside.
4. Prepare Quick Meat Broth and set aside to cool to lukewarm.
5. Dice bacon and place into the skillet.
6. Cook slowly, stirring frequently, until bacon is lightly browned. Remove bacon with slotted spoon and set aside. Add the beef to the bacon fat in the skillet. Cover skillet and cook over low heat 7 to 10 min., or until thoroughly heated.
7. Meanwhile, melt fat in a small saucepan over low heat.
8. Blend flour into the fat.
9. Heat until mixture bubbles, stirring constantly. Remove from heat and gradually add the reserved broth, stirring constantly. Return to heat and bring rapidly to boiling, stirring constantly; cook 1 to 2 min. longer. Remove saucepan from heat. Stirring vigorously with a French whip, whisk beater or fork, add sour cream to contents of saucepan in very small amounts.
10. Blend lemon juice, lemon peel and sugar into sauce.
11. Pour sauce over the meat. Return the bacon to skillet. Cook the mixture over low heat about 3 to 5 min., stirring constantly, until throughly heated; do not boil.

About 4 servings

Veal-Rice Casserole

1	lb. veal round cutlets, cut ¼ in. thick
¼	cup butter or margarine
1	tablespoon paprika
¼	cup hot water
1	teaspoon salt
2	qts. water
1	tablespoon salt
1	cup uncooked rice
½	lb. mushrooms
3	tablespoons butter or margarine
1	large or 2 small firm tomatoes
1½	cups thick sour cream
¼	cup grated Parmesan cheese

1. Grease a 2-qt. casserole; set out a large, heavy skillet having a tight-fitting cover.
2. Have veal round cutlets ready.
3. Cut veal into 1-in. pieces and set aside.
4. Heat butter or margarine in the large skillet over low heat.
5. Stir in paprika.
6. Place meat into skillet and brown over medium heat, stirring occasionally, Add water and salt.
7. Cover skillet and simmer about 45 min., or until meat is tender when pierced with a fork.
8. Meanwhile, bring to boiling water and salt in a deep saucepan.
9. So boiling will not stop, add uncooked rice gradually to water. (The Rice Industry no longer considers it necessary to wash rice before cooking).
10. Boil rapidly, uncovered, 15 to 20 min., or until a rice kernel is entirely soft when pressed between fingers. Drain rice in colander or sieve and rinse with hot water to remove loose starch. Cover colander and rice with towel and set over hot water until kernels are dry and fluffy.
11. Meanwhile, clean and slice mushrooms.
12. Melt butter or margarine in an 8-in. skillet over low heat.
13. Add the mushrooms to the butter. Stirring gently, cook over low heat until mushrooms are lightly browned and tender. Put contents of skillet into a bowl. Add the rice and gently mix with a fork. Set aside.
14. Wash and cut off and discard stem ends from tomatoes.
15. Cut tomatoes into ½-in. slices and set aside.
16. Place one half of meat into the casserole. Top with one-half rice-mushroom mixture and all of tomato slices. Repeat layering of meat and mushroom-rice mixture; top with a layer of sour cream.
17. Sprinkle grated Parmesan cheese over the sour cream.
18. Bake at 350°F about 15 to 20 min., or until thoroughly heated. Served immediately.

About 6 servings

Browned Veal

8	slices bacon, diced
½	cup (about 1 medium-size) chopped onion
¼	cup chopped green pepper
1½	teaspoons paprika
1½	lbs. boneless veal shoulder
¼	cup all-purpose flour
1	teaspoon salt
¼	teaspoon pepper
⅓	cup hot water

1. Place bacon, onion, green pepper and paprika into a heavy 10-or 12-in. skillet having a tight-fitting cover.
2. Cook slowly, stirring frequently, until bacon is lightly browned.
3. Meanwhile, cut boneless veal shoulder into 1-in. cubes.
4. Coat meat by shaking it in a plastic bag containing a mixture of flour, salt and pepper.
5. With slotted spoons, remove bacon mixture to small dish, leaving bacon fat in the skillet. Add meat to skillet and brown meat slowly on all sides.
6. Return bacon mixture to skillet with water.
7. Cover skillet and simmer, stirring occasionally and adding small amounts of water as needed, 45 to 60 min., or until meat is tender when pierced with a fork. Transfer the meat and liquid to warm platter or bowl and garnish with parsley.

About 4 to 6 servings

Veal Balls with Sour Cream

	Noodles (page 17)
1	lb. ground veal
¾	cup milk
½	cup (about 1½ slices) fine, dry bread crumbs
½	cup (about 1 medium-size) chopped onion
2	tablespoons chopped parsley
1	egg, well beaten
1	teaspoon salt
¼	teaspoon pepper
¼	cup fat
½	cup (4 oz. can) sliced mushrooms
½	cup Quick Meat Broth
1	cup thick sour cream

1. Prepare noodles.
2. Shortly before noodles are dry, set out heavy 10-in. skillet having a tight-fitting cover.
3. Lightly mix together ground veal, dry bread crumbs, onion, parsley, egg and a mixture of salt and pepper.
4. Form veal mixture into medium (2-in.) or small (1-in.) balls and set aside. Heat fat in the skillet.
5. Add veal balls to fat; brown over medium heat, turning balls occasionally. Add mushrooms.
6. Cover skillet and simmer 30 to 45 min., or until veal balls are done, turning balls occasionally and adding small amounts of water if needed.
7. Meanwhile, cook the noodles and drain.
8. Prepare Quick Meat Broth.
9. Set broth aside to cool to lukewarm.
10. When veal balls are done, remove skillet from heat. Drain cooking liquid off the meat into a cup; set skillet aside.
11. Place sour cream into top of a double boiler.
12. Add gradually to sour cream, stirring constantly, the liquid drained from skillet and the reserved broth.
13. Cook sauce over simmering water, stirring occasionally, until heated thoroughly.
14. Place noodles into serving bowl, top with contents of skillet and sour cream sauce. Serve immediately.

6 servings

Veal Paprika

Browned Veal (page 25)
Spatzle (see Chicken
Paprika with Spatzle, page
34)
1 tablespoon fat
1 tablespoon all-purpose
flour
2 teaspoons paprika
½ cup milk
1 cup thick sour cream

1. Prepare browned veal.
2. While veal is cooking, prepare spatzle and set aside in warm place.
3. Shortly before veal is tender, melt fat in a small saucepan over low heat.
4. Blend flour and paprika into the fat until smooth.
5. Heat until mixture bubbles, stirring constantly. Remove from heat and gradually add milk stirring constantly.
6. Return to heat and bring rapidly to boiling stirring constantly; cook 1 to 2 min. longer. Remove from heat. Stirring sauce vigorously with a French whip, whisk beater or fork, add sour cream in very small amounts.
7. When veal is tender, pour sauce into the skillet. Cook mixture over low heat, stirring constantly, 3 to 5 min., or until thoroughly heated; do not boil. Serve the Veal Paprika with the Spatzle.

4 to 6 servings

Lamb Chops with Dill Sauce

3 tablespoons fat
½ cup (about 1 medium-size) chopped onion
4 lamb shoulder chops, cut ½ in. thick
2 tablespoons water
1 tablespoon vinegar
1 teaspoon salt
¼ teaspoon pepper
1 bay leaf
½ cup Quick Meat Broth
2 tablespoons butter or margarine
2 tablespoons all-purpose flour
¼ teaspoon salt
Few grains pepper
1 tablespoon chopped fresh dill
½ cup dry white wine, such as Chablis or sauterne
2 tablespoons vinegar

1. For Chops—Melt fat in a large, heavy skillet having a tight-fitting cover.
2. Add onion to fat and, stirring occasionally, cook slowly about 5 min.
3. Remove onion from skillet with slotted spoon to small dish and set aside.
4. Have ready lamb shoulder chops.
5. Cut through fat on outside edges about every inch. Be careful not to cut through lean. Place chops in skillet; slowly brown both sides.
6. Meanwhile, mix together water, vinegar, salt, pepper and bay leaf.
7. Slowly add this mixture to the browned lamb. Return onion to skillet. Cover skillet and simmer 25 to 30 min., or until lamb is tender when pierced with a fork. If needed, add small amounts of water as lamb cooks.
8. For Sauce—When meat is almost tender, prepare Quick Meat Broth and set aside to cool to lukewarm.
9. Melt butter or margarine in small skillet over low heat.
10. Blend flour, salt and pepper into butter until smooth.
11. Heat until mixture bubbles and is lightly browned. Remove skillet from heat. Add gradually, stirring constantly, a mixture of the reserved broth and fresh dill.
12. Bring rapidly to boiling, stirring constantly; cook 1 to 2 min. longer. Remove sauce from heat and gradually add dry white wine and vinegar.
13. Serve the sauce over lamb chops.

4 servings

Lamb with Green Beans

2 lbs. boneless lamb shoulder
4 slices bacon, diced
½ cup (about 1 medium-size) chopped onion
2 teaspoons salt
1 teaspoon caraway seeds
1 teaspoon paprika
2 cups Quick Meat Broth
1 lb. (about 3 cups) green beans
½ cup liquid (reserved bean cooking liquid plus water)
¼ cup all-purpose flour
½ cup thick sour cream

1. Set out a heavy 10-in. skillet having a tight-fitting cover.
2. Put boneless lamb shoulder on a wooden cutting board and cut into 1-in. cubes.
3. Place bacon into the skillet.
4. Cook slowly, moving and turning frequently, until bacon is lightly browned. Remove bacon wirh slotted spoon to a small dish and set aside.
5. Add onion to the bacon fat in skillet.
6. Cook slowly, stirring occasionally, until onion is tender. Remove onion with slotted spoon to dish containing the bacon and set aside.
7. Add the meat to the bacon fat and brown slowly on all sides. Sprinkle over meat a mixture of salt, caraway seeds and paprika.
8. Remove skillet from heat and slowly pour in Quick Meat Broth.
9. Return bacon and onion to skillet. Cover skillet and simmer 1½ to 2 hrs., or until meat is tender when pierced with a fork.
10. About an hour before meat is tender, wash, remove ends, cut into 1-in. pieces and cook green beans 15 to 30 min., or until just tender.
11. If necessary, drain beans (reserving any cooking liquid) and set aside. Cool the cooking liquid.
12. Pour liquid into a small screw-top jar.
13. Sprinkle flour onto the liquid.
14. Cover jar tightly and shake until mixture is well blended. Bring contents of skillet to boiling. Slowly pour the flour mixture (shaking again if necessary) into skillet while stirring constantly. Bring this gravy to boiling, stirring constantly; cook 3 to 5 min. longer. Remove from heat and vigorously stir about ½ cup of the gravy, 1 tablespoon at a time, into sour cream.
15. Pour the mixture gradually into the skillet, stirring constantly. Gently mix in the green beans. Cook ingredients over low heat, moving mixture gently, 3 to 5 min., until heated thoroughly; do not boil.

About 5 to 7 servings

Beef with Green Beans: Follow recipe for Lamb with Green Beans. Substitute lean **beef** for lamb.

Ham Strudel

Strudel Dough (page 62)
3 cups finely chopped, cooked ham
¼ cup thick sour cream
½ teaspoon pepper
¼ cup (about 1 slice) fine, dry bread crumbs

1. Prepare strudel dough.
2. While dough is resting 30 min., thinly slice and finely chop cooked ham.
3. Mix ham with sour cream and pepper.
4. Set ham mixture aside.
5. After strudel dough is stretched and slightly dried, sprinkle dry bread crumbs evenly over the dough.
6. Spoon ham mixture in small mounds evenly over the dough. spread mounds carefully with spatula.
7. Roll, bake and slice as in Strudel (do not sprinkle with confectioners' sugar). Serve Ham Strudel warm.

8 to 10 servings

Lamb Casserole

2	lbs. lamb (cut in 1" cubes)
¼	cup oil
2	onions, chopped
1	clove garlic, minced
½	lb. peas
½	lb. string beans
6	carrots, scraped
½	head cauliflower
3	cups stewed tomatoes
¼	cup red wine

1. In a skillet heat the oil and brown the lamb on all sides.
2. Add onions and garlic and heat until onions are soft.
3. In a separate saucepan blanch the peas, string beans, carrots and cauliflower.
4. In a 2 quart casserole combine the wine, tomatoes and meat and bake in a 325°F oven for 1 hour.
5. Add the vegetables and continue cooking covered for another 15 minutes.

6 servings

Hungarian Pepperdish

4	large red or green peppers
1	lb. ground pork or beef
1	onion, chopped
¾	cup tomatoes
1	clove garlic, chopped
1	teaspoon salt
½	teaspoon pepper
1	teaspoon paprika
¾	cup cooked, cold rice
4	tablespoons grated cheese
1¼	cups water

1. Clean peppers and cut off tops. Remove seeds and veins. Place in an ovenproof dish.
2. Mix meat, onions, tomatoes and seasonings. Mix in rice and fill peppers with mixture. Sprinkle with cheese.
3. Pour water in bottom of dish so peppers don't burn on the bottom. Bake in a 350°F oven about 30 minutes till peppers are soft. Serve warm with cold sour cream.

4 servings

Frankfurters with Green Pepper and Tomatoes

¼	cup butter
4	medium-size green peppers, cut in lengthwise strips
2	medium-size onions, thinly sliced
4	large, ripe tomatoes (or use 1½ cups, 16-oz. can, drained, tomatoes)
1½	teaspoons salt
¼	teaspoon paprika
⅛	teaspoon freshly ground pepper
8	frankfurters

1. Melt butter in a large, heavy skillet, having a tight-fitting cover.
2. Add green peppers and onions to butter and cook until onion is almost tender, stirring occasionally.
3. Meanwhile, rinse tomatoes; cut out and discard stem ends and blemishes; cut into slices.
4. Add tomatoes to the skillet. Sprinkle a mixture of salt, paprika and ground pepper over the vegetables.
5. Cover skillet and simmer 15 min.
6. Meanwhile, cut frankfurters into 1-in. pieces.
7. Add frankfurters to skillet and mix gently with the vegetables; cover skillet and cook about 10 min. or until frankfurters are heated.

6 or 7 servings

Egg, Green Pepper and Tomato Scramble:
Follow recipe for Frankfurters with Green Pepper and Tomatoes. Omit frankfurters. After simmering 15 min., add 6 **eggs,** slightly beaten. Cook slowly over low heat, gently stirring occasionally with a fork or spatula, until eggs are thick and creamy throughout, but moist.

Gypsy-Style Fried Ham Slices

2	smoked ham slices, cut ¼ to ½ in. thick
1½	cups Quick Meat Broth (1½ times recipe, page 9)
2	tablespoons reserved fat
3	tablespoons (½ slice) fine, dry bread crumbs
4	teaspoons vinegar
1	teaspoon sugar few grains pepper
1	tablespoon chopped parsley

1. Lightly grease a heavy 10- or 12-in. skillet.
2. Cut through fat at 1-in. intervals on outside edges of smoked ham slices. Be careful not to cut through the lean.
3. Place ham into the skillet and cook slowly over medium heat 10 to 12 min., turning occasionally, until lightly browned on both sides.
4. Meanwhile, prepare Quick Meat Broth and set aside to cool to lukewarm.
5. Remove ham to heated platter, cover and set aside in warm place.
6. Pour off and reserve fat from skillet. Return fat to skillet.
7. Stir dry bread crumbs into fat and brown lightly, stirring constantly.
8. Remove skillet from heat and gradually add a mixture of the reserved broth, vinegar, sugar and pepper.
9. Bring mixture to boiling, stirring constantly. Blend in parsley.
10. Pour sauce over ham slices and serve immediately.

4 to 5 servings

Cabbage Strudel

1	head (about 3 lbs.) cabbage (about 3 qts. shredded)
2	tablespoons salt Strudel Dough (page 62)
¼	cup butter
¾	to 1 teaspoon pepper
¼	cup thick sour cream
¼	cup (about 1 slice) fine, dry bread crumbs

1. Set out a 3-qt. saucepan.
2. Remove and discard wilted outer leaves, rinse, cut cabbage into quarters (discarding core) and finely shred.
3. Place cabbage into a large bowl and mix with salt.
4. Let stand ½ hr., mixing occasionally.
5. Meanwhile, prepare Strudel Dough.
6. While Strudel Dough is resting 30 min., melt butter in the saucepan.
7. Squeeze cabbage, a small amount at a time, discarding the juice; put cabbage into the saucepan. Cook uncovered over medium heat, stirring frequently, 10 to 15 min., or until just tender. Remove cabbage from heat and mix in pepper.
8. Set cabbage aside.
9. After Strudel Dough is stretched and slightly dried, spoon sour cream over entire surface in small mounds.
10. Carefully spread mounds of cream with spatula. Sprinkle over the sour cream, dry bread crumbs.
11. Spoon cabbage in small mounds over the bread crumbs. With spatula spread mounds carefully.
12. Roll, bake and slice as in Strudel recipe (page 62; do not sprinkle with confectioners' sugar). Serve warm.

12 slices strudel

Sausage with Cabbage

1	head (about 2 lbs.) cabbage (about 2 qts., shredded)
1	qt. boiling water
1	teaspoon salt
2½	cups canned tomatoes
10	(about 2 lbs.) thuringer sausages
⅓	cup fat
1	tablespoon chopped onion
⅓	cup all-purpose flour
½	cup water

1. Set out a 4-qt. sauce pot having a tight-fitting cover.
2. Remove and discard wilted outer leaves of cabbage, rinse, cut into quarters (discarding core) and coarsely shred.
3. Place cabbage into sauce pot and add water and salt.
4. Cook cabbage, uncovered, over medium heat 10 min. Stir in contents of canned tomatoes.
5. Place on top of cabbage thuringer sausage links.
6. Cover sauce pot and cook 15 to 20 min., or until sausage is heated. Remove ½ cup cooking liquid from sauce pot and set aside to cool to lukewarm.
7. Meanwhile, make a thickening mixture by melting fat in a small skillet over low heat.
8. Add onion to the fat and cook until almost tender, stirring occasionally.
9. Blend in flour.
10. Stirring constantly, cook until mixture bubbles and is lightly browned. Remove from heat. Add water gradually, stirring constantly, a mixture of the ½ cup reserved cooking liquid and ½ cup water.
11. Remove the sausage from the sauce pot to serving platter. Immediately blend contents of skillet into liquid in sauce pot. Bring mixture rapidly to boiling, stirring constantly; cook 1 to 2 min. longer.
12. Serve sausage with some of cabbage mixture.

5 or 6 servings

Sweatbreads with Mushrooms

2	pairs lamb or veal sweetbreads
	Cold water
1	tablespoon vinegar or lemon juice
1½	teaspoon salt
1	10-oz. pkg. frozen peas
2	cups Quick Meat Broth (page 9)
½	lb. mushrooms
⅓	cup butter or margarine
3	tablespoons butter or margarine
3	tablespoons all-purpose flour
⅛	teaspoon pepper
4	egg yolks, slightly beaten

1. Set out a 2-qt. saucepan having a tight-fitting cover and a heavy, 10-in. skillet.
2. As soon as possible when purchased, rinse with cold water and place lamb or veal sweetbreads in saucepan.
3. Immediately cover with water.
4. Add 1 tablespoon vinegar or lemon juice and 1 tablespoon salt for each quart of water.
5. Cover saucepan and simmer 20 min. Drain sweetbreads; immediately cover with cold water. Drain sweetbreads again. (Cool and refrigerate now if sweetbreads are not to be used immediately.) Remove membrane. Separate sweetbreads into smaller pieces; set aside.
6. Cook frozen peas according to directions on package.
7. Meanwhile, prepare quick meat broth and set aside.
8. Clean and slice mushrooms.
9. Heat butter or margarine in the skillet.
10. Add mushrooms to butter and cook slowly, stirring gently until lightly browned and tender. Push mushrooms to one side. Melt butter or margarine in skillet.
11. Thoroughly blend into butter a mixture of flour, salt and pepper.
12. Heat until mixture bubbles and is lightly browned, stirring

constantly. Remove from heat and gradually add reserved broth, stirring constantly. Blend in mushrooms. Return to heat and bring rapidly to boiling, stirring constantly. Cook 1 to 2 min. longer. Vigorously stir about ⅓ cup hot mixture, 1 tablespoon at a time into egg yolks.

13. Immediately and thoroughly blend into mixture in skillet, stirring constantly. Cook 2 or 3 min. over low heat, stirring constanly. Mix in the drained peas and sweetbreads. Heat thoroughly, but do not boil. Serve immediately.

4 or 5 servings

Fish-Potato Casserole

6	medium-size (about 2 lbs.) potatoes
2	lbs. fish fillets, such as pike or trout
1	teaspoon salt
¼	teaspoon pepper
½	cup butter or margarine
⅓	cup hot milk
1	teaspoon salt
1	teaspoon paprika
⅛	teaspoon pepper
1¼	cups thick sour cream
¼	cup (about 1 slice) fine, dry bread crumbs
3	tablespoons finely chopped onion
2	tablespoons grated Parmesan cheese Paprika

1. Butter an 11x7x1½-in. baking dish. Set out a large, heavy skillet.
2. Wash, pare and cut potatoes into halves.
3. Cook potatoes 20 to 30 min., or until tender when pierced with a fork.
4. A few minutes before the potatoes are tender, set out fish fillets, such as pike or trout.
5. (If fish is frozen, thaw according to directions on package.) Cut into serving-size pieces. Sprinkle fish with a mixture of salt and pepper.
6. Set aside.
7. Heat butter or margarine in the skillet over low heat.
8. Place fish into skillet and lightly brown on both sides; carefully turn only once. Cook 8 to 10 min., or until fish flakes (can be separated with a fork into thin, layer-like pieces).
9. Drain potatoes. To dry potatoes, shake pan over low heat. Mash or rice potatoes. Whip into the potatoes butter or margarine.
10. Add gradually, whipping in a mixture of hot milk, salt, paprika and pepper.
11. Whip potato mixture until light and fluffy. Spread in bottom of baking dish.
12. Set out thick sour cream and dry bread crumbs.
13. Spread one-third of the sour cream over potatoes. Add a layer of onion.
14. Sprinkle onions with 3 tablespoons of the bread crumbs. Arrange fish in layers on top of crumbs. Sprinkle with remaining crumbs and grated Parmesan cheese.
15. Spread remaining sour cream over cheese. Sprinkle with paprika.
16. Bake at 350°F 20 to 30 min., or until thoroughly heated. Serve immediately.

6 servings

Sausage-Potato Casserole: Follow recipe for Fish-Potato Casserole. Substitute 10 (about 2 lbs.) **thuringer sausage links** for fish. To prepare sausage links, cook covered, in water to cover, over medium heat about 15 min.

Panfried Fish Fillets

2　lbs. fish fillets, such as pickerel, sole or haddock
2　cups (about 6 slices) fine, dry bread crumbs
1　teaspoon salt
¼　teaspoon pepper
2　eggs
1　tablespoon milk
¾　cup butter or margarine
¼　cup lemon juice
2　tablespoons finely chopped parsley

1. Set out a 10-in. skillet.
2. Have ready fish fillets, such as pickerel, sole or haddock.
3. (If fish is frozen, thaw according to directions on package.) Cut into serving-size pieces and set aside.
4. Mix dry bread crumbs, salt and pepper in a shallow pan or on waxed paper and set aside.
5. Beat eggs and milk slightly in a shallow bowl.
6. Heat butter or margarine in the skillet over low heat.
7. Dip fillets into eggs mixture; then coat with crumb mixture. Lightly brown both sides of fillets in the butter, turning only once. Cook only until fish flakes (can be separated with fork into thin, layer-like pieces). Transfer fish to warm serving platter, scraping loose and removing the bits of fish which have stuck to the skillet. Cover fish to keep warm.
8. Heat butter or margarine in the skillet.
9. Stir in lemon juice and parsley.
10. Heat thoroughly and pour over fish. Serve immediately.

5 or 6 servings

Fish Paprika

4　lbs. assorted fresh water fish (such as trout, pike and bass)
3　large (1 to 1½ lbs.) onions
2　qts. water (or enough to cover contents)
1　tablespoon paprika
2　teaspoons salt

1. Set out a 4-qt. kettle having a tight-fitting cover.
2. Clean and wash fresh water fish, such as trout, pike and bass in cold salted water.
3. (If fish is frozen, thaw according to directions on package.) Cut into 2-in. pieces.
4. Cut onions into slices ¼ in. thick.
5. Cover bottom of kettle with one layer of onion slices; add a layer of fish. Alternate in layers, remaining onion slices and fish. Add water to the kettle.
6. Bring to boiling; reduce heat to simmer and season fish with paprika and salt.
7. Cover kettle and simmer 30 to 40 min., or until fish flakes (can be separated with a fork into thin, layer-like pieces). Shake pan gently from time to time during cooking; do not stir. Remove fish from kettle with slotted spoon to large serving bowl or soup tureen. Strain the broth over fish. Serve hot in bowls.

About 8 servings

Poached Fish with Horseradish Sauce

1½	lbs. fish fillets, such as perch or bass
	Boiling water (enough to just cover fish)
½	cup dry white wine
1	small onion, chopped
2	tablespoons chopped parsley
1	teaspoon salt
⅛	teaspoon pepper
1	cup thick sour cream
3	tablespoons prepared horseradish
2	tablespoons grated lemon peel

1. Set out a 10-in. skillet having a tight-fitting cover. Also have ready a large square of cheesecloth.
2. For Poached Fish—Set out fish fillets, such as perch or bass.
3. (If fish is frozen, thaw according to directions on package.) Tie fish loosely in cheesecloth to prevent breaking; place into skillet. Add water, dry white wine, onion, parsley salt and pepper in order.
4. Cover skillet and simmer about 10 min., or until fish flakes (can be separated with a fork into thin, layer-like pieces). Meanwhile, prepare sauce.
5. For Horse-radish Sauce—Blend well sour cream, horseradish and lemon peel.
6. Pour sauce into serving dish; set aside.
7. Drain fish; remove cheesecloth. Place fish onto warm platter. Serve with sauce.

4 servings

Strawberry Pancakes

1	qt. fully ripe strawberries
1¼	cups sifted all-purpose flour
⅛	teaspoon salt
2	eggs, well beaten
½	cup milk
½	teaspoon vanilla extract
2	egg whites
4	teaspoons sugar
2	tablespoons sugar
	Confectioners' sugar

1. Set out a griddle or a heavy 10-in. skillet.
2. Wash and remove blemishes from strawberries.
3. Set 18 berries aside to garnish serving plates; hull and slice remaining berries, place them into refrigerator.
4. Sift together flour and salt into a bowl and set aside.
5. Beat with rotary beater to blend eggs, milk and vanilla extract.
6. Set griddle over low heat.
7. Make a well in center of dry ingredients. Add egg mixture, stirring batter only until blended; set batter aside.
8. Beat egg whites until frothy.
9. Add 4 teaspoons of sugar gradually, beating well after each addition.
10. Beat until stiff peaks are formed. Carefully fold egg whites into batter.
11. Test griddle; it is hot enough for baking when drops of water sprinkled on surface dance in small beads. Lightly grease griddle if manufacturer so directs. For each pancake pour about 1 cup of the batter onto griddle. Immediately tilt griddle back and forth to spread batter evenly. If necessary, use spatula to spread batter. Cook until pancake is puffy, full of bubbles and golden brown on underside. Turn only once and brown other side. Transfer pancakes to a warm platter and keep them warm by placing between folds of absorbent paper in a 350°F oven.
12. When all the pancakes are cooked, remove strawberries from refrigerator. Mix one-half of the sliced berries with sugar.
13. Spoon about ½ cup of the sweetened strawberries onto each pancake and roll. Place pancakes onto individual plates. Sprinkle each with confectioners' sugar.
14. Arrange remaining sliced strawberries over the top of pancakes. Garnish plates with leaf lettuce and the whole strawberries. Serve immediately.

3 servings

Chicken Paprika with Spatzle

1	frying chicken, 2 to 3 lbs., ready-to-cook weight
1	qt. hot water
1	small onion
3	parsley sprigs
2	teaspoons salt
3	peppercorns
1	bay leaf
8	slices bacon
¼	cup finely chopped onion
¾	cup all-purpose flour
1½	teaspoons salt
1½	teaspoons paprika
2	tablespoons fat
2	tablespoons all-purpose flour
1	cup reserved giblet broth
⅔	cup milk
1½	tablespoons paprika
1½	cups thick sour cream
2	qts. water
2	teaspoons salt
2⅓	cups sifted all-purpose flour
1	teaspoon salt
1	egg, slightly beaten
1	cup water
¼	cup butter or margarine, melted

1. For Chicken Paprika—Set out a deep, heavy 10-in. skillet (or a Dutch oven) having a tight-fitting cover.

2. Clean, rinse chicken and pat dry with absorbent paper.

3. Disjoint and cut into serving-size pieces. (If chicken is frozen, thaw according to directions on package.) Cut away and discard tough lining from gizzard. Slit heart; remove blood vessels. Refrigerate chicken and liver. Place cleaned gizzard, heart and neck into a saucepan and add water, onion, parsley sprigs, salt, peppercorns and bay leaf.

4. Bring water to boiling. Skim off and discard foam. Cover saucepan tightly and simmer 1 hr., or until giblets and neck meat are tender when pierced with fork.

5. Shortly before end of cooking period, dice bacon and place into the skillet.

6. Cook slowly, stirring and turning frequently, until bacon is slightly crisp and browned. Add chopped onion.

7. Stirring occasionally, cook until onion is almost tender.

8. Meanwhile, coat chicken evenly by shaking 2 or 3 pieces at a time in a plastic bag containing a mixture of flour, salt and paprika.

9. With slotted spoon, remove bacon and onion from skillet, leaving bacon fat in skillet. Set aside.

10. Slightly increase heat under the skillet. Starting with meaty pieces of chicken, brown skin sides first. Put in less meaty pieces as others brown. To brown on all sides, turn chicken pieces as necessary with two spoons or tongs. When chicken is lightly and evenly browned, reduce heat.

11. Add cooked gizzard, heart and neck to the skillet with 1 or 2 tablespoons of the giblet broth. (Strain remainder of broth; reserve 1 cup and cool to lukewarm.) Cover skillet tightly. Add liver to skillet 10 to 15 min. before end of cooking time. Cook chicken slowly 25 to 40 min., or until thick pieces are tender when pierced with a fork.

12. Meanwhile, melt fat in a small saucepan over low heat.

13. Blend flour into the fat.

14. Heat until mixture bubbles, stirring constantly. Remove from heat and add reserved giblet broth gradually, stirring constantly.

15. (If giblets are not being used, substitute 1 cup Quick Chicken Broth, page 9, for giblet broth.) Return saucepan to heat and bring mixture rapidly to boiling, stirring constantly; cook 1 to 2 min. longer. Gradually add milk and paprika to sauce, stirring constantly.

16. When thoroughly heated, remove saucepan from heat. Stirring vigorously with a French whip, whisk beater, or fork, add sour cream to the sauce in very small amounts.

17. Mix in the bacon and onion. Pour the sauce into the skillet over each piece of chicken. Cook the mixture over low heat, stirring sauce and turning chicken frenquently, 3 to 5 min., until thoroughly heated; do not boil. Cover skillet tightly; turn off heat under chicken and let stand about 1 hr. About twice during hour spoon sauce over chicken. Reheat just before serving.

18. For Spatzle (Drop Noodles)—After setting chicken and sauce aside, bring to boiling water and salt in a 3-or 4-qt.

saucepan.

19. Meanwhile, sift together flour and salt and set aside.

20. Combine in a bowl and mix together egg and water.

21. Gradually add flour mixture to egg mixture, stirring until smooth. (Batter should be very thick and break from a spoon instead of pouring in a continuous stream.) Spoon batter into the boiling water by ½ teaspoonfuls, dipping spoon into water each time. Cook only one layer of noodles at one time; do not crowd. After noodles rise to the surface, boil gently 5 to 8 min., or until soft when pressed against side of pan with spoon. Remove from water with slotted spoon, draining over water for a second, and place into a warm bowl. Toss noodles lightly with butter or margarine.

22. Place chicken onto a platter, leaving room at one end of platter for noodles. Cover chicken with sauce; sprinkle with paprika. Arrange noodles on platter. Garnish with parsley.

4 to 6 servings

Fried Chicken

1	**frying chicken, 2 to 3 lbs., ready-to-cook weight**
¾	**cup all-purpose flour**
1½	**teaspoons salt**
½	**teaspoon pepper**
1	**egg, slightly beaten**
1	**tablespoon water**
1	**cup (about 3 slices) fine, dry bread crumbs**
	Fat (or use cooking oil) to at least ½-in. depth
2	**tablespoons water**

1. Set out a Dutch oven or a heavy 12-in. skillet having a tight-fitting cover.

2. Clean, rinse chicken, and pat dry with absorbent paper.

3. (If chicken is frozen, thaw according to directions on package.) Disjoint and cut into serving-size pieces. Cut away and discard tough lining from gizzard. Slit heart; remove blood vessels. Refrigerate the liver. (For cooking of giblets and neck see Chicken Paprika with Spatzle, page 34.) To coat chicken evenly, shake 2 or 3 pieces at a time in a plastic bag containing a mixture of flour, salt and pepper.

4. Dip chicken pieces into a mixture of egg and water.

5. Roll chicken pieces in dry bread crumbs.

6. Let stand 5 to 10 min. to "seal" coating.

7. Meanwhile, melt fat in the skillet over medium heat.

8. Starting with meaty pieces of chicken, brown skin-sides first. Put in less meaty pieces as others brown. To brown all sides, turn pieces as necessary with two spoons or tongs. When chicken is evenly browned, reduce heat and add water.

9. Cover skillet and cook slowly 25 to 40 min., or until thick pieces are tender when pierced with a fork; uncover last 10 min. to crisp skin. Serve on a warm platter.

3 or 4 servings

Vegetables & Salads

Summer Squash with Dill

2	lbs. summer squash
½	cup boiling water
2	teaspoons finely chopped fresh dill or ¼ teaspoon dill seeds
½	teaspoon salt
1	cup thick sour cream
1	tablespoon lemon juice
2	teaspoons sugar
½	teaspoon paprika

1. Set out a 3-qt. heavy saucepan having a tight-fitting cover.
2. Wash squash, trim off ends and cut into thin crosswise slices. (Choose young, tender squash; it is not necessary to pare them. Pare the squash before slicing if the outside seems tough.)
3. Put squash into the saucepan with boiling water, dill seeds and salt.
4. Cover saucepan and simmer squash 15 to 20 min., or until just tender.
5. Meanwhile, heat sour cream, lemon juice, sugar and paprika thoroughly in top of double boiler over simmering water, stirring constantly.
6. Carefully mix sauce with the squash.
7. Serve immediately.

6 servings

Paprika Potatoes

4	medium-size (about 1 lb.) potatoes (about 2½ cups, cubed)
2	tablespoons bacon fat
¾	cup (about 1 large) chopped onion
1	teaspoon paprika
1	teaspoon salt
⅛	teaspoon pepper
1¼	cups thick sour cream
1	tablespoon chopped parsley

1. Set out a heavy 10-in. skillet having a tight-fitting cover.
2. Wash, pare and cut potatoes into ½-in. cubes.
3. Set potatoes aside.
4. Heat fat in the skillet.
5. Add onion to the bacon fat and cook over low heat, stirring occasionally, until almost tender.
6. Add to onion a mixture of paprika, salt and pepper.
7. Remove skillet from heat and blend sour cream into the fat and onion, stirring vigorously.
8. Add potatoes to sour cream mixture and mix gently and thoroughly. Cover skillet and cook over low heat, about 30 min., or until potatoes are just tender. Do not boil. Occasionally turn potatoes in sauce. Garnish with parsley.

4 to 6 servings

Potatoes with Tomato

6   medium-size (about 2 lbs.) potatoes
1/4   cup butter
1/4   cup chopped onion
1   cup (8-oz. can) tomato sauce
1   tablespoon sugar
1/8   teaspoon pepper
1   cup thick sour cream
1/2   cup milk
2   tablespoons chopped parsley

1. Wash and cook potatoes 20 to 30 min., or until tender when pierced with a fork.
2. Drain the potatoes. To dry potatoes, shake pan over low heat. Peel and slice 1/4 in. thick; set aside in warm place.
3. Melt butter over heat in the saucepan in which potatoes were cooked.
4. Add onion to the butter and cook until almost tender, stirring frequently.
5. Mix tomato sauce, sugar and pepper with the onions and heat to boiling.
6. Remove saucepan from heat. Stirring vigorously with a French whip, whisk beater or fork, add sour cream and milk to contents of saucepan in very small amounts.
7. Gently mix potatoes into the sauce and cook over low heat, stirring constantly, 3 to 5 min., until heated thoroughly; do not boil.
8. Garnish with parsley.
9. Serve immediately.

6 to 8 servings

Carrots Cooked in Butter

8   medium-size carrots (about 2 cups, sliced)
1/4   cup butter or margarine
2   teaspoons finely chopped parsley
1   teaspoon sugar
1/2   teaspoon salt
1   cup Quick Meat Broth (page 9)
1/4   cup water
2   tablespoons all-purpose flour

1. Set out a heavy 2-qt. saucepan having a tight-fitting cover.
2. Cut off and discard tops; wash, pare or scrape carrots, and cut into 1/4-in. slices.
3. Set carrots aside.
4. Melt butter or margarine in the saucepan over low heat.
5. Add the carrots to butter with parsley, sugar and salt.
6. Cover saucepan and cook about 20 min., or until carrots are just tender, stirring occasionally to coat evenly and prevent scorching.
7. Meanwhile, prepare quick meat broth and set aside.
8. Put 1/4 cup water into a small, screw-top jar.
9. Sprinkle all-purpose flour into the water.
10. Cover jar tightly and shake until ingredients are well blended. Set aside.
11. Remove carrots from saucepan with slotted spoon to a warm bowl; cover bowl.
12. Pour the reserved broth into the saucepan in which carrots were cooked. Return saucepan to heat. Again shake jar containing flour-water mixture and gradually add mixture to the broth stirring constantly. Bring broth rapidly to boiling, stirring constantly; cook 3 to 5 min. longer. Pour this sauce over carrots.

4 to 6 servings

Green Beans

1 lb. green beans
1 cup Quick Meat Broth (page 9)
3 tablespoons butter
3 tablespoons all-purpose flour
2 tablespoons vinegar or lemon juice
1 to 2 tablespoons sugar
¼ teaspoon paprika

1. Wash green beans, break off ends and cut into 1-in. pieces.
2. Cook beans 15 to 20 min., or until beans are tender.
3. Meanwhile, prepare quick meat broth and set aside to cool to lukewarm.
4. Melt butter in a small skillet over low heat.
5. Blend all-purpose flour into butter.
6. Heat until mixture bubbles and is lightly browned, stirring constantly. Remove skillet from heat. Gradually add the reserved broth, stirring constantly. Return to heat and bring rapidly to boiling, stirring constantly; cook 1 to 2 min. longer. Remove skillet from heat.
7. Stir vinegar or lemon juce and sugar into sauce.
8. Cover skillet and set sauce aside.
9. When beans are tender, pour sauce over beans and simmer 5 min. Turn beans into bowl and sprinkle with paprika.

About 4 servings

Deep-Fried Cauliflower with Sour Cream Sauce

1 medium-size head cauliflower
2 egg yolks, slightly beaten
1 cup thick sour cream
2 teaspoons lemon juice
½ teaspoon salt
¼ teaspoon paprika
¼ teaspoon pepper
Hydrogenated vegetable shortening, all-purpose shortening, lard or cooking oil for deep-frying
⅔ cup (2 slices) fine, dry bread crumbs
½ teaspoon salt
¼ teaspoon pepper
2 eggs, slightly beaten
¼ cup milk

1. Remove leaves, cut off all the woody base and trim off any blemishes from cauliflower.
2. Carefully break into 5 or 6 flowerets. Allow cauliflower to stand in cold salted water a few mins. to remove dust or small insects.
3. Rinse cauliflower and cook 20 to 30 min. or until tender but still firm. Meanwhile, prepare sauce.
4. Mix together in top of double boiler egg yolks, sour cream, lemon juice, salt, paprika and pepper.
5. Cook over simmering water, stirring constantly, 3 to 5 min., or until sauce is thoroughly heated. Set aside and keep warm.
6. About 20 min. before deep-frying, fill a deep saucepan one-half to two-thirds full with hydrogenated vegetable shortening, all-purpose shortening, lard or cooking oil for deep-frying.
7. Heat slowly to 365°F. When using automatic deep-fryer, follow manufacturer's directions for the amount of fat and timing.
8. Drain cauliflower and set aside to cool slightly.
9. Meanwhile, mix dry bread crumbs, salt and pepper.
10. Blend together eggs and milk.
11. Dip flowerets into egg mixture and then into the crumb mixture. Deep-fry only one layer of flowerets at one time; do not crowd. Fry them 2 to 4 min., or until golden brown, turning occasionally. Drain flowerets over fat for a few seconds before removing to absorbent paper. Place cauliflowerets into bowl and top with the Sour Cream Sauce. Serve immediately.

4 to 6 servings

Batter-Fried Cauliflower: Follow recipe for Deep-Fried Cauliflower With Sour Cream Sauce. Omit egg and bread crumb mixtures. Beat together with rotary beater flour, milk, egg and salt for a batter coating. Dip cooked cauliflowerets into batter and deep-fry.

Baked Cauliflower

1 large head cauliflower
½ cup (about 1½ slices) buttered fine, dry bread crumbs
½ cup grated Parmesan cheese
2 egg yolks, slightly beaten
2 tablespoons all-purpose flour
2 cups thick sour cream
2 egg whites
1 cup cubed cooked ham

1. Lightly grease a 1½-qt. casserole.
2. Remove leaves and cut off all the woody base from large head of cauliflower.
3. Trim off any blemishes. Carefully break into flowerets and allow cauliflower to stand in cold, salted water for a few min. to remove dust or small insects.
4. Rinse cauliflower and cook 20 to 30 min., or until tender but firm.
5. Mix together bread crumbs and Parmesan cheese and set aside.
6. Mix together egg yolks, all-purpose flour in a bowl.
7. Blend into egg yolk mixture thick sour cream.
8. Beat egg whites until stiff, not dry, peaks are formed.
9. Fold egg whites into sour cream mixture. Set sauce aside.
10. Drain cauliflower; arrange one-half on bottom of casserole.
11. Spoon over cauliflowerets cubed cooked ham.
12. Pour one-half of the sauce over ham. Arrange remaining cauliflower over sauce; then add sauce. Sprinkle crumb mixture over top.
13. Bake at 350°F 20 to 30 min., or until top is lightly browned.

6 to 8 servings

Creamed Chopped Spinach

1 pkg. (10 oz.) frozen chopped spinach
2 tablespoons butter or margarine
2 tablespoons all-purpose flour
¼ teaspoon salt
⅛ teaspoon garlic salt
⅛ teaspoon freshly ground pepper
¾ cup cream
1 egg, slightly beaten

1. Thaw spinach partially and cook in a heavy 2-qt. saucepan.
2. Meanwhile, melt butter or margarine in a small saucepan over low heat.
3. Blend flour, salt, garlic salt and pepper into the butter until smooth.
4. Heat until mixture bubbles, stirring constantly. Remove from heat. Add cream gradually, stirring constantly.
5. Return to heat and bring rapidly to boiling, sitrring constantly; cook 1 to 2 min. longer. Remove sauce from heat. Vigorously stir about 3 tablespoons sauce into egg.
6. Immediately blend this mixture into hot sauce, stirring until smooth. Cover sauce and set aside in a warm place.
7. When spinach is tender, drain in sieve, pressing spinach firmly against sieve with back of spoon to remove water thoroughly.
8. Blend spinach into sauce. Serve hot.

About 4 servings

Creamed Garden-Fresh Spinach: Follow recipe for Creamed Chopped Spinach substituting 1½ lbs. **fresh spinach** for frozen spinach. Remove and discard tough stems, roots and bruised leaves from spinach. Wash leaves thoroughly by lifting up and down several times in a large amount of cold water. Lift leaves out of water each time before pouring off water. When free from sand and gritty material, transfer spinach to large, heavy saucepan. Add 1 clove **garlic.** Cook 8 to 10 min. Omit garlic salt in the sauce. When spinach is tender, discard garlic. Drain spinach as in recipe. Finely chop spinach and drain again; combine with sauce.

Asparagus with Sour Cream

2 lbs. asparagus
½ cup Quick Meat Broth (page 9)
1 tablespoon butter
1 tablespoon all-purpose flour
½ teaspoon salt
¼ teaspoon pepper
1 egg yolk, slightly beaten
1 cup thick sour cream

1. Break off and discard lower parts of stalks as far down as they will snap from asparagus.
2. Wash asparagus thoroughly. If necessary, remove scales to dislodge any sand. Cook 10 to 20 min., or until asparagus is just tender.
3. Meanwhile, for sauce, prepare Quick Meat Broth, and set aside.
4. Melt butter in a small skillet over low heat.
5. Blend flour, salt and pepper into the butter until smooth.
6. Heat until mixture bubbles, stirring constantly. Remove skillet from heat. Gradually add the broth, stirring constantly. Return to heat and bring rapidly to boiling, stirring constantly; cook 1 to 2 min. longer. Remove sauce from heat. Vigorously stir about 3 tablespoons of hot sauce into egg yolk.
7. Immediately blend into hot mixture. Stirring sauce constantly, cook slowly 2 to 3 min. (Do not overcook or allow sauce to boil.) Remove from heat. Stirring vigorously with a French whip, whisk beater or fork, add sour cream to sauce in very small amounts.
8. Cook sauce over low heat, stirring constantly, 3 to 5 min., until heated thoroughly. Do not boil sauce; remove immediately from heat. Cover saucepan and set sauce aside.
9. Drain asparagus and cut stalks into 3 or 4 pieces; put into bowl. Pour sauce over asparagus and blend lightly.

6 to 8 servings

Cabbage with Caraway Seeds

1 head (about 2 lbs.) red or green cabbage (about 2 qts., shedded)
⅓ cup butter
1 teaspoon caraway seeds
1 teaspoon salt
⅛ teaspoon pepper
2 tablespoons vinegar

1. Set out a heavy 3-qt. saucepan having a tight-fitting cover.
2. Remove and discard wilted outer leaves, rinse, cut into quarters and coarsely shred cabbage.
3. Melt butter in the saucepan.
4. Add the cabbage to butter with a mixture of caraway seeds, salt and pepper.
5. Cover the saucepan and cook over low heat, stirring frequently, 10 to 15 min., or until cabbage is just tender. Stir vinegar into the cabbage mixture.
6. Cover saucepan and cook 5 min. longer.

About 6 servings

Mushrooms in Sour Cream

1 lb. mushrooms
½ cup Quick Meat Broth (page 9)
6 tablespoons butter
1 small onion, sliced
1 tablespoon butter
1 tablespoon all-purpose flour
½ teaspoon salt
⅛ teaspoon pepper
1 cup thick sour cream
2 tablespoons finely chopped parsley

1. Set out a 10-in. skillet.
2. Clean and slice mushrooms and set aside.
3. Prepare Quick Meat Broth and set aside.
4. Melt 6 tablespoons butter in the skillet.
5. Add the mushrooms to the butter with onion.
6. Cook slowly, stirring gently, until mushrooms are lightly browned and tender and onion is soft. Remove from heat and set aside.
7. Melt 1 tablespoon butter in a small saucepan.
8. Blend flour, salt and pepper into the butter until smooth.
9. Heat until mixture bubbles, stirring constantly. Remove from

heat. Gradually add the reserved broth, stirring constantly. Return to heat and bring rapidly to boiling, stirring constantly; cook 1 to 2 min. longer; remove from heat. Stirring vigorously with a French whip, whisk beater or fork, add sour cream to contents of saucepan in very small amounts.

10. Pour sour cream mixture into the skillet and place over low heat. Stirring constantly, but gently, heat thoroughly about 3 to 5 min.; do not boil. Blend parsley into contents of skillet.

11. Serve immediately.

4 to 6 servings

Cucumber Salad

2	medium-size (about 1¼ lbs.) cucumbers, washed and pared
2	teaspoons salt
3	tablespoons vinegar
3	tablespoons water
½	teaspoon sugar
¼	teaspoon paprika
¼	teaspoon pepper
½	clove garlic, minced
¼	teaspoon paprika

1. Slice cucumbers thinly into a bowl.
2. Sprinkle salt over the cucumber slices.
3. Mix lightly and set cucumbers aside for 1 hr.
4. Meanwhile, mix vinegar, water, sugar, ¼ teaspoon paprika, pepper and garlic together and set aside.
5. Squeeze cucumber slices, a few at a time (discarding liquid), and put into a bowl. Pour the vinegar mixture over the cucumbers and toss lightly together. Sprinkle ¼ teaspoon paprika onto cucumbers.
6. Chill the salad in refrigerator for 1 to 2 hrs.

6 to 8 servings

Cucumber Salad with Sour Cream: Follow recipe for Cucumber Salad. Blend in 1 cup **thick sour cream** after the vinegar mixture.

Cucumber Salad with Onions: Follow recipe for Cucumber Salad or variation. Omit garlic. Cut off root ends from 3 or 4 fresh **green onions or scallions.** Trim green tops down to 2- or 3-in., removing any wilted or bruised parts; peel and rinse. Slice onions by holding on hard surface and cutting across all with sharp knife. Add sliced onions to cucumber slices before adding the vinegar mixture.

Beet Salad

1 16	oz. can sliced beets (about 2 cups, drained)
½	cup vinegar
¼	cup reserved beet liquid
2	tablespoons sugar
1½	teaspoons salt
1	teaspoon caraway seeds
⅛	teaspoon freshly ground pepper

1. Drain contents of can sliced beets, reserving liquid.
2. Place the beets into a 1-qt. bowl and add a mixture of vinegar, beet liquid, sugar, salt, caraway seeds, and pepper.
3. Toss beets lightly in this salad marinade. Cover bowl and place into refrigerator to marinate 1 or 2 days; carefully turn beets occasionally.
4. Serve beets with some of the marinade.

4 or 5 servings

Beet Salad with Horse-radish: Follow recipe for Beet Salad. Add 1 or 2 tablespoons **freshly grated horse-radish** or ¼ cup **prepared horse-radish** to beets with the seasonings.

Lettuce Salad

3	hard-cooked eggs
1	large head lettuce
6	slices bacon
½	cup vinegar
¼	cup reserved bacon fat
¼	cup water
3	tablespoons sugar
½	teaspoon salt

1. Prepare eggs.
2. Meanwhile, cut out core and discard buised leaves from lettuce, rinse with cold water and drain well.
3. Cut into 6 wedges. Set aside in refrigerator.
4. Dice and panbroil bacon, reserving bacon fat.
5. Set bacon aside for garnish.
6. Put vinegar, bacon fat, water, sugar and salt into the skillet.
7. Heat mixture to boiling, stirring well. Place lettuce wedges on salad plates. Pour vinegar mixture over lettuce wedges.
8. Peel and slice the eggs and use as a garnish with the bacon.

6 servings

Tomato Salad

¼	cup vinegar
¼	cup olive oil
2	tablespoons sugar
¼	teaspoon salt
⅛	teaspoon pepper
5	medium-size tomatoes
½	cup (about 1 meduim-size) chopped onion
2	tablespoon chopped parsley

1. Combine vinegar, olive oil, sugar, salt and pepper in a small, screw-top jar; cover tightly and chill in refrigerator.
2. Rinse tomatoes and dip into boiling water for a few seconds.
3. Peel tomatoes, cut out and discard stem ends and chill thoroughly in refrigerator. Cut the tomatoes into small pieces and put into salad bowl with onion and chopped parsley.
4. Shake jar of dressing until well blended and pour over salad; lightly toss together. Serve immediately.

4 or 5 servings

Tomato Salad with Green Pepper: Follow recipe for Tomato Salad. Substitute for parsley, 1 **green Pepper** chopped (about ½ cup, chopped).

Green Bean Salad

1	9 oz. pkg. frozen French-style green beans Oil-Vinegar Marinade (page 44)
4	slices bacon

1. Cook frozen French-style green beans.
2. Drain beans thoroughly and put into a bowl; set aside to cool.
3. Meanwhile, prepare Oil-Vinegar Marinade.
4. Pour marinade over beans. Gently toss beans until well coated with marinade. Chill beans in refrigerator about 1 hr.; carefully turn beans occasionally.
5. Shortly before serving, panbroil bacon.
6. Crumble bacon and set aside.
7. Drain beans thoroughly, and put into a bowl. Carefully mix the beans with the bacon.

3 or 4 servings

Green Bean Salad with Onion: Follow recipe for Green Bean Salad. Add 1 tablespoon finely chopped **onion** to green bean-bacon mixture.

Potato Salad with Sour Cream Dressing

8   (about 2½ lbs.) medium-
    size potatoes
¾   cup (about 1½ medium-
    size) chopped onion
½   cup chopped celery
⅓   cup vinegar
1½ teaspoons paprika
1   teaspoon salt
⅛   teaspoon pepper
2   cups thick sour cream
¼   cup butter

1. Wash and cook potatoes 20 to 30 min., or until potatoes are tender when pierced with a fork.
2. Drain potatoes. To dry potatoes, shake pan over low heat. Peel potatoes, cut into cubes and put into a large bowl. (The cubed potatoes will measure approximately 6 cups.) Add to the potatoes onion, chopped celery and a mixture of vinegar, paprika, salt and pepper.
3. Toss ingredients together lightly with a fork; let stand 15 min.
4. Meanwhile, heat sour cream and butter in top of a double boiler over simmering water until butter is melted.
5. Stir until sour cream and butter are well blended and pour over potato mixture, mixing carefully with a fork to blend well. Chill thoroughly in the refrigerator before serving.
6. Garnish with parsley.

6 to 8 servings.

Potato-Onion Salad

6   medium-size (about 2 lbs.)
    potatoes
1   large onion
    Oil-Vinegar Marinade
    (page 44)
1   green pepper

1. Wash, cook potatoes 20 to 30 min., or until potatoes are tender when pierced with a fork.
2. Drain potatoes. To dry potatoes, shake pan over low heat. Set aside to cool.
3. Meanwhile, thinly slice onion and separate into rings.
4. Peel potatoes and cut into ¼-in. slices.
5. Arrange potatoes and onion rings alternately in a large shallow dish and add Oil-Vinegar Marinade.
6. Chill at leat 1 hr. in the refrigerator, carefully turning vegetables occasionally.
7. Shortly before serving the salad, rinse and remove the stem end of green pepper.
8. Remove all white fiber and seeds from the pepper; rinse the cavity. Cut green pepper crosswise into 1/8-in. rings and set aside.
9. Pour the marinade off the potatoes and onions before serving. Garnish top of the salad with the green pepper rings.

About 6 servings

Potato-Onion Salad With Eggs: Follow recipe for Potato-Onion Salad. Prepare 2 or 3 **Hard-Cooked Eggs.** Slice eggs and place on top of salad with green pepper rings. Sprinkle lightly with **paprika.**

Cabbage Salad

1	head (about 2 lbs.) cabbage (about 2 qts., shredded)
1	tablespoon salt
1/3	cup wine vinegar
3	tablespoons salad oil
1	tablespoon sugar
1/8	teaspoon freshly ground pepper
1/4	cup chopped onion
1/4	cup chopped green pepper
2	medium-size tomatoes

1. Remove and discard wilted outer leaves, rinse cabbage, cut into quarters (discarding core) and finely shred.
2. Place cabbage into a large bowl and toss with salt.
3. Let mixture stand 1 hr., tossing occasionally.
4. Meanwhile, combine wine vinegar, salad oil, sugar and ground pepper in a small screw-top jar and set aside.
5. Squeeze the cabbage, a small amount at a time, and discard the juice. Place cabbage into salad bowl and add onion and green pepper.
6. Shake the dressing until well blended and pour over the salad. Using salad spoon and fork, turn and toss cabbage mixture until well coated with dressing.
7. Rinse tomatoes and dip into boiling water for a few seconds.
8. Peel; cut out and discard stem ends and cut each tomato into eighths. Arrange tomatoes over top of salad.
9. Chill salad in refrigerator 1 hr. before serving.

6 to 8 servings

Oil-Vinegar Marinade

1/2	cup vinegar
2	tablespoons olive oil
1	tablespoon sugar
1	teaspoon salt
1/2	teaspoon freshly ground pepper

1. Put vinegar, olive oil, sugar, salt and ground pepper into a small screw-top jar.
2. Cover tightly and shake jar until ingredients are well blended.
3. If marinade is not used immediately, store in refrigerator and beat or shake thoroughly before serving.

About 2/3 cup

Fruit Salad

2	cups any mixture of fresh fruits, such as watermelon balls, sliced bananas, peach or pear cubes, berries, pitted cherries, seeded or seedless grapes or orange sections
1/4	cup sifted confectioners' sugar
	Lettuce cups
4	teaspoons rum, cognac or wine

1. Put any mixture of fresh fruits into a small bowl.
2. (Dip banana, peach and pear pieces into lemon juice to prevent darkening.) Add confectioner's sugar to fruit and toss gently.
3. Chill fruit in refrigerator 1 hr. Toss salad gently. Spoon individual portions into lettuce cups.
4. Serve on chilled salad plates.
5. Set out rum, cognac or wine.
6. Sprinkle 1 teaspoon over each salad. Serve immediately.

4 servings

Cantaloupe Salad

2   **medium-size, ripe can-taloupes**
½   **cup mayonnaise**
½   **cup thick sour cream**
½   **teaspoon salt**
⅛   **teaspoon pepper**

1. Rinse and cut ripe cantaloupes into halves.
2. Remove seedy centers and pare. Cut cantaloupes into ¾-in. cubes, put into a large bowl and set aside.
3. For Dressing—Mix together mayonnaise, sour cream, salt and pepper until well blended.
4. Pour one-half of the dressing onto cantaloupe and toss lightly until well mixed. Chill cantaloupe and remaining dressing in the refrigerator for about 1 hr. Remove from refrigerator and place individual servings on crisp lettuce on chilled salad plates. Top each serving with some remaining dressing.

About 8 servings

Eggs

Mushroom Omelet

¾ lb. mushrooms
¼ cup butter or margarine
¼ cup all-purpose flour
½ teaspoon salt
⅛ teaspoon pepper
1 cup milk
3 eggs, slightly beaten
4 teaspoons butter or margarine

1. Set out an 8-in. skillet and a round 8 or 9-in. shallow baking dish.
2. Clean and slice mushrooms.
3. Heat ¼ cup butter or margarine in the skillet over low heat.
4. Add mushrooms to the butter and cook them slowly, stirring gently, until lightly browned and tender. Reserve about 8 mushroom slices for top of omelet. Place remaining mushrooms and liquid into a bowl; cover bowl and set it aside in a warm place. Set the skillet aside.
5. Melt butter or margarine in a small saucepan over low heat.
6. Blend all-purpose flour, salt and pepper into the butter until smooth.
7. Heat until mixture bubbles. Remove saucepan from heat. Add milk gradually, stirring constantly.
8. Return to heat and bring rapidly to boiling, stirring constantly. Remove from heat. Vigorously stir about ⅓ cup of the hot mixture, 1 tablespoon at a time, into eggs.
9. Immediately blend into remaining hot mixture, stirring until smooth. Cover and set aside.
10. Place the skillet over low heat.
11. Meanwhile, measure 4 teaspoons butter or margarine.
12. Test skillet; it is hot enough when drops of water sprinkled on surface dance in small beads. Reduce heat under skillet and melt 1 teaspoon of the butter in the skillet. Pour about one-fourth of the egg mixture into the skillet and cook over low heat until it is lightly browned on bottom and firm but slightly moist on top. Loosen edges carefully with spatula and slide the omelet layer into the baking dish.
13. Remove about one-third of mushrooms with slotted spoon and spread over the omelet layer. Repeat process with remaining egg mixture, alternating omelet and mushroom layers. Top the last omelet layer with reserved mushroom slices.
14. Bake at 350°F 10 to 15 min., or until omelet is thoroughly heated. Cut omelet into wedges; garnish with parsley.

4 servings

Mushroom Omelet with Onions: Follow recipe for Mushroom Omelet. Combine with sliced mushrooms ½ cup (about 1 medium-size) chopped **onion** and 2 tablespoons chopped **green pepper.** Cook until onions are tender, stirring occasionally.

Egg Croquettes

4	hard-cooked eggs
¼	cup butter or margarine
½	all-purpose flour
1	teaspoon salt
	Few grains pepper
2	cups milk
3	eggs, slightly beaten
	Mushroom-Wine Sauce (see Deep-Fried Eggs with Mushrooms-Wine Sauce, page 48)
	Hydrogenated vegetable shortening, all-purposose shortening, lard or cooking oil for deep-frying
1½	cups (4 or 5 slices) fine, dry bread crumbs
1	egg, well beaten
1	tablespoon milk

1. Prepare hard-cooked eggs.
2. Meanwhile, melt butter or margarine over direct heat in top of a 1-qt. double boiler.
3. Blend into the butter a mixture of all-purpose flour, salt and pepper.
4. Heat until mixture bubbles, stirring constantly. Remove from heat. Add milk gradually, stirring constantly.
5. Return to heat and bring rapidly to boiling, stirring constantly; cook 1 to 2 min. longer. Remove from heat. Vigorously stir about ¼ cup of the hot sauce, 1 tablespoon at a time, into eggs, slightly beaten.
6. Quickly blend into sauce. Cook over simmering water 3 to 5 min., stirring slowly to keep it cooking evenly. Remove sauce from simmering water and cool slightly by setting double boiler top in bowl of cold water.
7. Peel and dice the hard-cooked eggs and gently mix them with the sauce. Cool completely and chill mixture in the refrigerator 1 hr. or longer.
8. Before shaping the croquettes, prepare Mushroom-Wine Sauce and keep warm.
9. About 20 min. before deep-frying fill a deep saucepan one-half to two-thirds full with hydrogenated vegetable shortening, all-purpose shortening, lard or cooking oil for deep-frying.
10. Heat slowly to 375°F. When using an automatic deep-fryer, follow manufacturer's directions for amount of fat and timing.
11. Shape cold egg mixture into croquettes (balls or cones), using about ¼ cup of mixture for each. Roll them in dry bread crumbs.
12. Then dip them into a mixture of egg and milk.
13. Again roll them in bread crumbs. Shake off loose crumbs. Deep-fry croquettes 3 to 5 min., or until golden brown. Fry only one layer of croquettes at a time; do not crowd. Turn them occasionally to brown evenly. Remove croquettes with slotted spoon, draining over fat for a second. Remove to absorbent paper.
14. Serve with the Mushroom-Wine Sauce.

12 croquettes

Potato and Egg Casserole

6   hard cooked eggs
7   medium-size (about 2 lbs.) potatoes
⅓   cup fine, dry buttered crumbs
1   cup thick sour cream
½   cup butter, melted and cooled
     Salt and pepper

1. Generously butter a 2-qt. casserole.
2. Pepare hard-cooked eggs.
3. Meanwhile, wash potatoes.
4. Cook about 25 to 30 min., or until potatoes are tender. Drain potatoes. To dry potatoes, shake pan over low heat. Peel. Cut potatoes and eggs into ¼-in. slices and set aside.
5. Prepare dry buttered crumbs and set aside.
6. Mix together sour cream and butter.
7. Reserve one-half of the sour cream mixture for top of casserole.
8. Beginning and ending with potatoes, alternate three layers of potatoes and two layers of eggs in the casserole; spoon about 6 tablespoons sour cream mixture over each egg layer and season with salt and pepper.
9. Cover top layer of potatoes with reserved sour cream mixture. Sprinkle with the buttered crumbs.
10. Bake at 350°F 20 to 30 min., or until crumbs are browned.

6 or 7 servings

Deep Fried Eggs with Mushroom-Wine Sauce

1   cup Quick Meat Broth
½   lb. mushrooms
6   tablespoons butter
3   tablespoons finely chopped onion
2   tablespoons finely chopped parsley
3   tablespoons butter
3   tablespoons all-purpose flour
¾   teaspoon salt
⅛   teaspoon pepper
¾   cup dry white wine
     Hydrogenated vegetable shortening, all-purpose shortening, lard or cooking oil for deep-frying
10   hard-cooked eggs
1⅓   cups sifted all-purpose flour
½   teaspoon salt
2   eggs, slightly beaten
¼   cup milk

1. For Mushroom-Wine Sauce—Set out an 8-in. skillet.
2. Prepare Quick Meat Broth and set aside.
3. Clean mushrooms and slice.
4. Melt 6 tablespoons butter in skillet over low heat.
5. Add the mushrooms to the butter with chopped onion and parsley.
6. Cook slowly, stirring gently, until mushrooms are lightly browned and tender and onions are almost soft. Remove mushroom mixture and the liquid from skillet to a bowl; cover bowl and set aside.
7. Melt 3 tablespoons butter in the skillet.
8. Blend 3 tablespoons all-purpose flour, salt and pepper into butter until smooth.
9. Heat until mixture bubbles and is lightly browned. Remove from heat. Add gradually the reserve broth, stirring constantly. Return to heat and bring rapidly to boiling, stirring constantly; cook 1 to 2 min. longer.
10. Remove skillet from heat. Add dry white wine gradually to sauce, stirring constantly.
11. Mix the mushrooms and the liquid in bowl with the sauce in skillet; cover skillet and set aside.
12. For Eggs—About 20 min. before deep-frying, fill a deep saucepan one-half to two-thirds full with hydrogenated vegetable shortening, all-purpose shortening, lard or cooking oil for deep-frying.
13. Heat slowly to 365°F. When using automatic deep-fryer, follow manufacturer's directions for amount of fat and timing.
14. Prepare and remove shells from hard-cooked eggs.
15. For Batter—Sift together 1⅓ cups all-purpose flour and salt and set aside.
16. Combine 2 eggs and milk in a 1-qt. bowl.
17. Add to egg mixture enough of the flour mixture to make a

very stiff batter, stirring just until smooth.

18. Dry hard-cooked eggs thoroughly with absorbent paper. Cut two eggs into halves and wrap in waxed paper; set aside for garnish. Place remaining eggs into batter, a few at a time, to coat thoroughly. Carefully remove eggs from batter with fork or slotted spoon to the heated fat. Deep-fry eggs 3 to 4 min., or until golden brown. Fry only one layer of eggs at a time; do not crowd. Turn eggs occasionally to brown evenly. Rmeove eggs with slotted spoon, draining over fat for a second before removing to absorbent paper. Place the eggs on a warm platter. Garnish the platter with the reserved hard-cooked egg halves and parsley. Serve with the Mushroom-Wine Sauce.

4 servings

Baked Eggs with Sour Cream

1¾   **cups thick sour cream**
⅓   **cup (1 slice) fine, dry bread crumbs**
¼   **cup butter, cut in small pieces**
6   **eggs**
⅓   **cup grated Parmesan cheese**

1. Butter a 1½-qt. casserole.
2. Set out sour cream, dry bread crumbs and butter.
3. Place in the casserole 1¼ cups sour cream and one-half of butter. Sprinkle over sour cream and butter one-half of the crumbs.
4. Set out eggs.
5. Break one of the eggs into a saucer. Slip the egg onto bread crumbs by tilting saucer toward inside edge of casserole. Add each of the remaining eggs in the same way. Carefully arrange remaining butter, sour cream and crumbs over eggs. Top with grated Parmesan cheese.
6. Bake at 325°F 25 to 35 min., or until eggs are set. Serve immediately.

4 to 6 servings

Mushrooms with Scrambled Eggs

1   **lb. mushrooms**
½   **cup butter**
¼   **cup chopped onion**
2   **eggs, slightly beaten**
2   **tablespoons thick sour cream**
¼   **teaspoon salt
Few grains pepper**

1. Set out a 10-in. skillet.
2. Clean and slice mushrooms.
3. Heat butter in the skillet.
4. Add the mushrooms to butter with chopped onion.
5. Cook slowly, stirring occasionally, until onion is almost tender and mushrooms are lightly browned.
6. Meanwhile, blend eggs, sour cream, salt and pepper thoroughly.
7. Pour egg mixture into the skillet, mixing with the mushrooms and onions. Cook slowly over low heat; with a fork or spatula lift mixture from bottom and sides of skillet as it thickens, allowing uncooked part to flow to bottom. Avoid constant stirring. Cook until eggs are thick and creamy thoughout but still moist.

4 or 5 servings

Suet Pastry Crescents 66; Strawberry Pancakes 33; Cucumber Salad 41; Chicken Paprika with Spatzle 34

Scrambled Eggs with Anchovies

6	eggs, slightly beaten
6	tablespoons thick sour cream
⅛	teaspoon pepper
4	anchovy fillets, very finely chopped
3	tablespoons butter or margarine

1. Set out an 8-in. skillet.
2. Blend eggs, sour cream, pepper and anchovy fillets thoroughly in a mixing bowl.
3. Heat the skillet until just hot enough to sizzle a drop of water. Melt butter or margarine in the skillet.
4. Pour the egg mixture into the skillet and cook slowly over low heat. With a fork or spatula lift egg mixture from bottom and sides of skillet as it thickens, allowing uncooked part to flow to bottom; do not stir. Cook until eggs are thick and creamy throughout but still moist. Serve immediately.

4 servings

Brown Butter Eggs

⅓	cup butter
6	eggs
	Few grains salt
	Few grains pepper
½	teaspoon vinegar

1. Heat butter in a heavy 10-in. skillet until lightly browned.
2. Set out eggs.
3. Break one of the eggs into a saucer. Slip egg into the skillet by tilting saucer toward inside edge of the skillet. Add each of the remaining eggs in the same way. Reduce heat. Frequently basting eggs with butter in skillet, cook slowly, about 4 min., or until eggs reach desired stage of firmness. Or, instead of basting, cover pan; or turn eggs over once.
4. Sprinkle each egg with salt and pepper.
5. Remove eggs to warm platter. Add vinegar to remaining butter in skillet and mix well.
6. Pour vinegar-butter mixture over eggs and serve immediately.

4 to 6 servings

Desserts & Coffee Cakes

Linzer Torte

2¼	cups sifted all-purpose flour
1	cup unsalted butter
1⅓	cups sugar
8	egg yolks
8	egg whites
16	almonds
⅓	cup thick raspberry preserves
	Chocolate Frosting (see Sacher Torte, page 57)

1. Prepare two 9-in. round layer cake pans.
2. Measure all-purpose flour, divide into four portions and set aside.
3. Cream unsalted butter until very soft and fluffy.
4. Add sugar gradually, creaming until fluffy after each addition.
5. Add egg yolks one at a time, beating until very well blended and fluffy after each addition.
6. Beat an additional 2 min. after addition of final egg yolk. Set egg yolk mixture aside.
7. Beat egg whites until frothy.
8. Add 2 tablespoons of sugar at a time, beating well after each addition.
9. Continue beating until very stiff peaks are formed. Gently spread beaten egg whites over egg yolk mixture. Sift one portion of the flour over egg whites; gently fold with a few strokes until batter is only partially blended. Repeat with second and then third portions of flour. Sift remaining one-fourth of flour over batter and gently fold just until blended. Do not overmix! Gently turn batter into pans and spread to edges.
10. Bake at 350°F 30 to 35 min., or until torte tests done. Cool and remove from pans.
11. Meanwhile, blanch almonds and set aside.
12. When torte is cooled, spread raspberry preserves evenly over top of one layer.
13. Place second layer on top; set torte aside.
14. Prepare and frost sides and top of torte with Chocolate Frosting.
15. Before frosting becomes firm, garnish top edge of torte with the almonds.

12 to 16 servings

Dobos Torte

8   **hazelnuts**
4   **sq. (4 oz.) unsweetened chocolate**
1   **cup firm unsalted butter**
1   **teaspoon vanilla extract**
1   **cup sugar**
¼   **cup water**
6   **egg yolks**
1   **cup sifted all-purpose flour**
6   **egg yolks**
¼   **cup sugar**
6   **egg whites**
⅛   **teaspoon salt**
¼   **cup sugar**
¾   **cup confectioners' sugar**

1. Six 8-in. round layer cake pans or six 8-in. round layer cake pans with removable bottoms will be needed. (If necessary, three cake layers may be baked at one time and the same three pans reused for the remaining three layers.)

2. For Frosting—Put hazelnuts into a small shallow baking dish.

3. Roast at 400°F 3 to 5 min., or until skins are loosened and nuts are lightly toasted. Remove nuts from oven and cool slightly; discard skins. Finely chop or crush hazelnuts and set aside.

4. Melt unsweetened chocolate and set aside to cool.

5. Cream unsalted butter and vanilla extract in a large bowl until butter is light and fluffy and set bowl aside.

6. Mix sugar and water in a small saucepan having a tight-fitting cover.

7. Bring to boiling, stirring gently until sugar is dissolved. Cover saucepan and boil syrup gently 5 min. to help wash down any crystals that might have formed on sides of saucepan. Uncover saucepan and continue cooking syrup to thread stage (230°F to 234°F), or until syrup spins a 2-in. thread when allowed to drop from fork or spoon. (Remove from heat while testing.) Set syrup aside.

8. Meanwhile, beat eggs until thick and lemon colored.

9. Beating constantly with rotary beater, pour the hot syrup very gradually in a thin stream into egg yolks. (Do not scrape syrup from bottom and sides of saucepan.) Beat egg yolk mixture until very thick and of same consistency as the creamed butter. Cool completely. Beat egg yolk mixture, about 2 tablespoons at a time, into the butter until just blended. Gradually blend in the chocolate and the hazelnuts. Set frosting into the refrigerator to chill.

10. For Torte—Prepare the six 8-in. round layer cake pans or grease bottoms of the six 8-in. round layer cake pans with removable bottoms.

11. Measure all-purpose flour and set aside.

12. Put egg yolks and sugar into a large bowl and beat until very thick and lemon colored.

13. Set egg yolk mixture aside.

14. Beat egg whites and salt until frothy.

15. Add sugar gradually to egg whites, beating well after each addition.

16. Continue beating until very stiff peaks are formed. Gently spread egg yolk mixture over beaten egg whites.

17. Divide the sifted flour into four portions. Sift one portion at a time over egg mixture and gently fold just until bleded after each addition. Spoon equal amounts of batter into cake pans and spread ¼ in. thick. Stagger pans in oven.

18. Bake at 350°F about 15 min., or until lightly browned. Remove torte layers to cooling racks. If using waxed paper lined pans, carefully and quickly remove layers from pans. Beginning at center, tear paper and gently pull it off in small pieces. (Allow layers in removable bottom pans to stand in pans 2 min., loosen edges with spatula and carefully cut layers away from bottoms of pans.) Carefully place onto cooling racks right-side up and cool completely.

19. Beat the chilled frosting until fluffy. Spread frosting 1/8 in.

thick on four of the torte layers, placing one layer on top of another. Add fifth layer, but do not frost top. Thinly spread frosting on sides of torte. Put the five layers and remainder of frosting into refrigerator.

20. Meanwhile, place the sixth layer, which will be the top of torte, onto a shallow baking sheet. With back of knife blade, make 16 to 18 wedge-shape indentations on top of layer, but do not cut wedges apart. Grease a small area of baking sheet around torte layer (so that caramel topping will not stick to baking sheet if it runs off).

21. For Caramel Topping—Melt confectioners' sugar in heavy, light-colored, small skillet over low heat, stirring constantly.

22. Occasionally remove skillet from heat and press out lumps in sugar with back of spoon. Cook sugar until smooth and golden brown. Remove from heat and quickly pour onto top layer of torte. Spread caramel topping evenly over layer with a spatula, working rapidly before sugar hardens. With back of knife blade, make wedge-shape indentations over the ones made previously in the torte layer. With blade of knife, cut wedges apart.

23. Remove the layers and frosting from refrigerator. Beat frosting until fluffy. Spread frosting 1/8 in. thick on top of fifth layer and arrange caramel-topped wedges on top of it. Frost sides of sixth layer. Using a pastry bag and a No. 6 decorating tube, pipe a border of frosting around top edge of torte. Chill torte in refrigerator until frosting is firm. Cut servings with knife, blade of which has been dipped into hot water.

16 to 18 servings

Walnut Torte with Butter Frosting

½ cup sifted all-purpose flour

½ teaspoon concentrated soluble coffee

½ teaspoon cocoa or Dutch process cocoa

2 cups (about ½ lb.) walnuts (about 3½ cups, grated)

6 egg yolks

½ cup sugar

1 teaspoon grated lemon peel

1 teaspoon rum

½ teaspoon vanilla extract

6 egg whites

⅛ teaspoon salt

½ cup sugar

½ cup (about 2 oz.) walnuts (about ¾ cup, grated)

1½ cups firm unsalted butter

½ teaspoon vanilla extract

½ teaspoon rum

2 egg yolks

1 cup plus 2 tablespoons sugar

⅓ cup water

2 egg whites

1. Grease bottoms of two 9-in. round layer cake pans with removable bottoms or prepare two 9-in. round layer cake pans.
2. Sift together all-purpose flour, concentrated soluble coffee and cocoa or Dutch process cocoa.
3. Grate 2 cups walnuts.
4. Thoroughly combine walnuts with flour mixture, divide into four portions and set aside.
5. Beat 6 egg yolks and 1½ cups sugar until very thick and lemon colored.
6. Mix grated lemon peel, rum and vanilla extract gently into egg yolk mixture.
7. Set egg yolk mixture aside.
8. Beat 6 egg whites and salt until frothy.
9. Add sugar gradually to egg whites, beating well after each addition.
10. Continue beating until very stiff peaks are formed. Gently spread egg yolk mixture over beaten egg whites. Spoon one portion of the flour-walnut mixture over egg mixture and gently fold with a few strokes until batter is only partially blended. Repeat with second and then third portions. Spoon remaining one-fourth of flour-walnut mixture over batter and gently fold just until blended. Do not overmix! Gently turn batter into pans and spread to edges.
11. Bake at 350°F to 30 min., or until torte tests done. Cool and remove from pans as directed. When torte is cooled, prepare the frosting. Frost torte and place in refrigerator until ready to serve.
12. For Butter Frosting—Grate ½ cup walnuts and set aside.
13. Cream together unsalted butter, vanilla extract and rum until mixture is light and fluffy.
14. Add 2 egg yolks one at a time, beating thoroughly after each addition.
15. Set aside.
16. Combine sugar and water in a small saucepan having a tight-fitting cover.
17. Bring to boiling over medium heat, stirring gently until sugar is dissolved. Cover saucepan tightly and boil syrup gently 5 min. to help wash down any crystals that might have formed on the sides of saucepan. Uncover saucepan and continue cooking syrup to thread stage (230°F to 234°F), or until syrup spins a 2-in. thread when allowed to drop from spoon. (Remove pan from heat while testing.)
18. Meanwhile, beat 2 egg whites until stiff (but not dry) peaks are formed.
19. Continue beating egg whites and pour the hot syrup in a thin stream into beaten egg whites. (Do not scrape syrup from bottom and sides of pan.) Continue beating a few minutes just until egg white mixture is very thick (piles softly) and of same consistency as the butter mixture, Cool completely. Beat egg white mixture, about 2 tablespoons at a time, into butter mixture until just blended. Gradually blend the grated walnuts into frosting. If necessary, chill frosting in refrigerator until firm enough to spread.

12 to 16 servings

Hazelnut Torte: Follow recipe for Walnut Torte with Butter Frosting. Substitute 1½ cups (about ½ lb.) **hazelnuts** for walnuts.

Raspberry Whipped Cream Torte

1⅓ **cups sifted all-purpose flour**

3 **tablespoons unsalted butter**

6 **eggs**

4 **egg yolks**

1½ **cups sifted confectioners' sugar**

2 **cups red raspberries**

1 **teaspoon rum**

2 **cups whipping cream**

½ **cup sifted confectioners' sugar**

2 **teaspoons sugar**

1. Set out a 4-qt. double boiler or a 4-qt. heat resistant bowl and a large kettle.
2. Prepare two 9-in. round layer cake pans.
3. Measure all-purpose flour, divide into four portions and set aside.
4. Melt unsalted butter over simmering water and set aside to cool.
5. Put eggs, egg yolks and 1½ cups confectioners' sugar into top of double boiler.
6. Set over simmering water, making sure the bottom of double boiler top does not touch water. (Or, use the 4-qt. bowl set over the large kettle containing simmering water, making sure that bottom of bowl does not touch water.) With rotary beater, beat egg mixture constantly for about 5 min., or until mixture is slightly heated.
7. Remove double boiler top from simmering water and beat egg mixture until thick, piled softly and completely cooled. Sift one portion of the flour over egg mixture and gently fold with a few strokes until batter is only partially blended. Repeat with second and then third portions of flour. Sift remaining one-fourth of flour over batter and gently fold just until blended. Gradually add melted butter, folding just until blended. Do not overmix! Gently turn batter into pans and spread to edges.
8. Bake at 350°F 25 to 30 min., or until torte tests done. Cool and remove from pans as directed.
9. While torte is cooling, rinse and thoroughly drain red raspberries.
10. Select 16 berries for garnish and place in refrigerator.
11. Cut remaining raspberries and mix with rum.
12. Set fruit aside.
13. For Sweetened Whipped Cream—Chill in refrigerator two 1-qt. bowls, a rotary beater and whipping cream.
14. Set out ½ cup confectioners' sugar.
15. Pour 1 cup of chilled cream into each bowl. Beat until cream stands in peaks when beater is slowly lifted upright. With few final strokes, beat one-half the sugar into each portion of whipped cream. Place one half in refrigerator.
16. To Assemble Torte—Fold the cut raspberries into the second portion of whipped cream and spread evenly over one of the torte layers. Top with second layer; using spatula, cover sides and then top of torte with the reserved whipped cream.
17. Roll reserved berries in sugar.
18. Arrange raspberries in a circle around top edge of torte. Set into refrigerator until ready to serve. To avoid sogginess, chill torte no longer than 1 hr.

About 10 to 12 servings.

Cherry Torte

1	cup (about ⅓ lb.) almonds
2	tablespoons fine, dry bread crumbs
2	tablespoons sugar
1	lb. dark sweet cherries (about 2¼ cups, pitted)
6	egg yolks
3	tablespoons sugar
3	tablespoons lemon juice
6	egg whites
⅛	teaspoon salt
3	tablespoons sugar
3	egg whites
6	tablespoons sugar

1. Set out deep 9-in. spring-form pan.
2. Blanch almonds.
3. Grate ⅔ cup of the blanched almonds (about 1⅔ cups, grated); mix with dry bread crumbs.
4. Divide almond-crumb mixture into four portions and set aside. Toast and coarsely chop the remaining almonds; mix with 2 tablespoons sugar.
5. Reserve almond-sugar mixture for topping.
6. Wash, cut into halves and remove pits from dark sweet cherries.
7. Drain cherries and set aside.
8. Beat egg yolks, 3 tablespoons sugar and lemon juice in a large bowl until very thick and lemon colored.
9. Set egg yolk mixture aside.
10. Beat 6 egg whites and salt until frothy.
11. Add 3 tablespoons sugar gradually to egg whites, beating well after each addition.
12. Continue beating until very stiff peaks are formed. Gently spread egg yolk mixture over beaten egg whites. Spoon one portion of the almond-crumb mixture over egg mixture and gently fold with a few strokes until batter is only partially blended. Repeat with second and then third portions of almond-crumb mixture. Spoon remaining one-fourth of almond-crumb mixture over batter and gently fold just until blended. Do not overmix! Gently turn batter into pan and spread to edges. Gently place cherries evenly over top of batter.
13. Bake at 350°F 30 to 40 min., or until torte test done. Set torte onto cooling rack. Cool torte in pan 15 min. Remove the rim from the bottom of the pan and if desired, cut away torte from pan bottom and return to rack. When torte is completely cooled, set onto a baking sheet.
14. For Meringue—Beat 3 egg whites until frothy.
15. Add 6 tablespoons sugar gradually to egg whites, beating well after each addition.
16. Continue beating until stiff peaks are formed. Completely cover sides and top of torte with the meringue. Sprinkle the toasted almond mixture evenly over the top of the meringue.
17. Bake at 350°F 10 to 15 min., or until meringue is delicately browned. Cool torte and transfer to a cake plate. Before cutting first serving of torte, dip knife blade into hot water. To cut remainder of torte, (for each cut) wipe meringue off knife blade and dip knife blade into hot water.

12 to 16 servings

Sacher Torte

1	cup plus 2 tablespoons sifted all-purpose flour
4	oz. semi-sweet candymaking chocolate
½	cup unsalted butter
⅓	cup sugar
6	egg yolks
7	egg whites
⅓	cup sugar
⅓	cup strawberry preserves
⅓	cup strawberry jelly
3	oz. semi-sweet candymaking chocolate
½	cup unsalted butter

1. Prepare 11x7x1½-in. cake pan.
2. Measure all-purpose flour, divide into four portions and set aside.
3. Grate semi-sweet candymaking chocolate and set aside.
4. Cream unsalted butter until very soft and fluffy.
5. Add ⅓ cup sugar gradually, creaming until fluffy after each addition.
6. Add egg yolks one at a time, beating until very well blended and fluffy after each addition.
7. Set egg yolk mixture aside.
8. Beat egg whites until frothy.
9. Add ⅓ cup sugar gradually, beating well after each addition.
10. Continue beating until very stiff peaks are formed. Gently spread beaten egg whites over egg yolk mixture. Spoon the grated chocolate evenly over the egg whites. Sift one portion of the flour over the chocolate; gently fold with a few strokes until batter is only partially blended. Repeat with second and then third portions of flour: Sift remaining fourth of flour over batter and gently fold just until blended. Do not overmix! Gently turn batter into pan and spread to edges.
11. Bake at 350°F 25 to 30 min., or until torte tests done. Cool and remove from pan as directed. When torte is cooled, split into two layers. Spread strawberry preserves evenly over top of one layer (cut-side up).
12. Place second layer (cut-side down) on top of preserves and spread with strawberry jelly.
13. Prepare Chocolate Frosting.
14. For Chocolate Frosting—Partially melt semi-sweet candymaking chocolate being careful not to overheat.
15. Remove chocolate from the simmering water and stir until completely melted. Add unsalted butter.
16. Stir until butter is melted. Cool frosting slightly and pour onto torte; spread evenly over sides and top. Chill torte until frosting is firm.

About 12 servings

Filled Pancakes

Cottage Cheese Filling
(one half recipe, page 64)
or Nut Filling (one-half
recipe, page 64) or set out
1 to 1½ cups thick jam,
such as apricot or peach
1   cup sifted all-purpose
     flour
1½   teaspoons sugar
⅛   teaspoon salt
1   egg, slightly beaten
1   cup milk
½   teaspoon vanilla extract
Confectioners' sugar

1. Prepare filling and set aside.
2. For Batter—Set out a 6-in. skillet.
3. Sift together all-purpose flour, sugar and salt into a bowl.
4. Mix together egg, milk and vanilla extract.
5. Make a well in center of the dry ingredients and add milk mixture. Beat mixture with rotary beater until smooth.
6. Heat the skillet until moderately hot. Test skillet; it is hot enough when drops of water dance in small beads on surface. Lightly butter skillet. Remove skillet from heat; pour in 2 to 2½ tablespoons batter, or just enough batter to cover bottom of skillet. Immediately tilt skillet back and forth to spread batter thinly and evenly. (Batter should be very thin at all times so that it will spread easily. Stir in a small amount of additional milk from time to time because batter thickens on standing.)
7. Fry pancake over medium heat until lightly browned on bottom. Loosen edges with spatula. Turn pancake and brown second side; invert onto a warm plate. Repeat with remainder of batter, buttering skillet lightly for each pancake.
8. While one pancake is frying, spread baked pancake with 2 tablespoons filling; roll. Transfer to warm platter and keep pancakes warm by placing in a 350°F oven. Serve pancakes warm, sprinkle with confectioners' sugar.

14 to 16 pancakes

Pancakes Baked with Sour Cream: Follow recipe for Filled Pancakes. Omit confectioners' sugar. Place roll and filled pancakes one layer deep in buttered shallow baking dish about 13x9x2-in. Spoon 2 cups **thick sour cream** evenly over them. Bake uncovered at 350°F 25 to 30 min., or until thoroughly heated.

Poppy Seed Souffle

¼   cup (about 1 oz.) blanched
     almonds (about ¼ cup,
     chopped)
½   cup (about 2 oz.) freshly
     ground poppy seeds
¼   cup butter or margarine
¼   cup sugar
4   egg yolks, well beaten
¼   cup (about 1 slice) fine,
     dry bread crumbs
¼   cup milk
4   egg whites

1. Grease bottom of a 1-qt. baking dish.
2. Heat water for the hot water bath.
3. Finely chop almonds.
4. Mix almonds with ground poppy seeds.
5. Set mixture aside.
6. Put butter or margarine into a bowl and cream until softened.
7. Add sugar gradually, creaming until fluffy after each addition.
8. Add egg yolks in thirds beating thoroughly after each addition.
9. Mix in the poppy seed-almond mixture, dry bread crumbs and milk.
10. Beat egg whites until stiff, not dry peaks are formed.
11. Slide egg whites onto poppy seed mixture; quickly and gently fold together. Turn batter into baking dish. Set dish into the hot water bath.
12. Bake at 350°F 45 to 50 min., or until a silver knife, inserted halfway beween center and edge, comes out clean. Serve immediately.

5 to 6 servings

Sponge Puff Dessert

1⅓ **cups sifted all-purpose flour**
5 **egg yolks**
3 **tablespoons sugar**
1 **tablespoon water**
8 **egg whites**
⅛ **teaspoon salt**
3 **tablespoons sugar**
Rum Whipped Cream Dessert, Mocha Whipped Cream Dessert or Chocolate Whipped Cream Dessert, page 60
¾ **lb. milk chocolate or semi-sweet candymaking chocolate**

1. Cover baking sheets with unglazed paper and draw 2½-in. circles on it, spacing them about 2 in. apart.
2. Measure all-purpose flour and set aside.
3. Put egg yolks, 3 tablespoons sugar and water into a 1½-qt. bowl and beat until very thick and lemon colored.
4. Sift one-half of the flour, about 2½ tablespoons at a time, over egg yolk mixture and fold just until blended after each addition; set aside.
5. Beat egg whites and salt until frothy.
6. Add 3 tablespoons sugar gradually to egg whites, beating well after each addition.
7. Continue beating until very stiff peaks are formed. Gently spread egg yolk mixture over egg whites and fold until blended. Lightly sift one-half remaining flour over egg mixture and fold just until flour is blended. Sift remaining flour over batter and fold. Do not overmix!
8. Using drawn circles on the unglazed paper as a guide, quickly and gently spoon batter onto baking sheets in peaked mounds. Keep mounds as uniform as possible.
9. Bake at 325°F 15 to 20 min., or until slightly browned. With spatula, cut puffs away from paper and allow to cool on cooling rack. Hollow out centers from tops of one-half of puffs and from bottoms of remaining one-half. Tear portions taken from centers into small pieces; set aside.
10. Prepare Whipped Cream Dessert (but do not spoon into sherbet glasses).
11. Set 1 cup of the whipped cream dessert into the refrigerator; reserve for garnish. Fold the pieces taken from the puffs into remaining whipped cream and spoon into the hollows in the puffs. Use puffs having flat bottoms as bases. Top with remaining puffs so that the cream in base and cream in top puff come together. Place puffs flat onto cooling rack having waxed paper underneath. Set aside.
12. Partially melt milk chocolate or semi-sweet candymaking chocolate over simmering water, being careful not to overheat.
13. Remove chocolate from simmering water and stir until completely melted. Spoon chocolate onto puffs, allowing excess chocolate to drip onto waxed peper. Spread chocolate evenly over tops, if necessary. (Scrape together and wrap excess chocolate; store for future use.)
14. When chocolate is firm, place puffs onto individual plates. Using pastry bag and a No. 27 decorating tube, pipe reserved whipped cream around base of each puff. Serve immediately.

10 to 12 servings

Rum Whipped Cream Dessert

2 cups whipping cream
½ cup sifted Vanilla Confectioners' Sugar (below)
3 tablespoons rum

1. Put into refrigerator to chill, a 1-qt. bowl, a rotary beater and whipping cream.
2. Set out sifted vanilla confectioners' sugar and rum.
3. Pour 1 cup of chilled cream into the chilled bowl. Beat until cream stands in peaks when beater is slowly lifted upright; beat into whipped cream with final few strokes, one-half of the sugar and rum. Spoon lightly into four chilled sherbet glasses. Prepare remaining whipping cream following the same procedure. Serve immediately.

8 servings

Mocha Whipped Cream Dessert: Follow recipe for Rum Whipped Cream Dessert. Sift 2 tablespoons **concentrated soluble coffee** with sugar. Omit rum.

Cocoa Whipped Cream Dessert: Follow receipe for Rum Whipped Cream Dessert. Sift ⅓ cup **cocoa** with the sugar. Omit rum.

Vanilla Confectioners' Sugar

Confectioners' sugar
1 vanilla bean, about 9 in. long

1. Fill a 1- to 2-qt. container, having a tight-fitting cover, with confectioners' sugar.
2. Remove vanilla bean from air-tight tube, wipe with a clean, damp cloth and dry.
3. Cut vanilla bean into quarters lengthwise; cut quarters crosswise into thirds. Poke pieces of vanilla bean down into the sugar at irregular intervals. Cover container tightly and store on pantry shelf.

Note: The longer sugar stands, the richer will be the vanilla flavor. If tightly covered, sugar may be stored for several months. When necessary, add more sugar to jar. Replace vanilla bean when aroma is gone.

Noodles with Cottage Cheese and Bacon

Noodles (page 17); cut
noodles ¼ to ½ in. wide)
6 slices bacon
½ lb. (about 1 cup, firmly
packed) dry cottage
cheese
⅓ cup thick sour cream
¼ teaspoon salt
1 tablespoon butter, melted
1 tablespoon reserved bacon
fat

1. Prepare and cook noodles.
2. Meanwhile, panbroil bacon, reserving fat.
3. Crumble bacon and set aside.
4. Mix together cottage cheese, sour cream and salt, and set aside.
5. Put the drained noodles into a bowl and toss lightly with a mixture of melted butter and reserved bacon fat.
6. Top each serving of noodles with about 3 tablespoons of the cottage cheese mixture. Sprinkle with the crumbled bacon.

6 to 8 servings

Noodles with Nuts

Noodles (page 17; cut
noodles about ¼ in. wide)
1 cup (about 4 oz.) finely
chopped walnuts
⅓ cup confectioners' sugar
2 tablespoons butter,
melted
1 teaspoon lemon juice
½ teaspoon grated lemon
peel

1. Prepare and cook noodles.
2. Meanwhile, mix walnuts and confectioners' sugar together and set aside.
3. Place the drained noodles into a bowl and toss lightly with a mixture of melted butter, lemon juice, and lemon peel.
4. Carefully stir noodles with a fork until ingredients are well blended. Top each serving with some of the walnut-sugar mixture.

6 to 8 servings

Noodles with Poppy Seeds: Follow recipe for Noodles with Nuts. Increase melted butter to ¼ cup. Substitute ⅔ cup (about 3 oz.) freshly ground **poppy seeds** for walnuts.

Strudel

1	**tablespoon vinegar**
	Lukewarm (80°F to 85°F)
	water
4	**cups sifted all-purpose**
	flour
1	**egg, slightly beaten**
1	**tablespoon butter, melted**
	Melted Butter
½	**cup all-purpose flour**
	Egg, slightly beaten
2	**tablespoons confectioners'**
	sugar

1. Generously butter a 15½x10½x1-in. jelly roll pan.
2. *For Strudel Dough*—Place vinegar into a measuring cup for liquids.
3. Add water to the measuring cup up to the one-cup line.
4. Set liquid mixture aside.
5. Place flour into a large bowl and make a well in the center.
6. Add egg and 1 tablespoon butter to the flour.
7. Add the liquid mixture gradually to ingredients in the bowl, mixing until all flour is moistened. Turn dough out onto lightly floured pastry board and knead. Hold dough high above board and hit it hard against the board about 100 to 125 times, or until dough is smooth and elastic and small bubbles appear on the surface. Knead dough occasionally during the hitting process. Shape dough into a smooth ball and put onto lightly floured board. Lightly brush top of dough with melted butter.
8. Cover dough with an inverted bowl and allow it to rest 30 min.
9. Meanwhile, prepare and set aside one of the fillings (pages 63 and 64).
10. Cover a table (about 48x30-in.) with a clean cloth and sprinkle cloth evenly with approximately ½ cup all-purpose flour.
11. Place dough onto center of cloth and sprinkle dough very lightly with flour. Roll dough into rectangle ¼- to ⅛-in. thick.
12. Clench the fists, tucking the thumbs under the fingers. With the palm-side of fists down, reach under the dough to its center (dough will rest on back of hands). Being careful not to tear dough, stretch the center of the dough gently and steadily toward you as you slowly walk around the table. (Dough should not have *any* torn spots, if possible, but such perfection will come with practice.)
13. As the center becomes as thin as paper, concentrate the stretching motion closer to the edge of the dough. Continue until dough is as thin as tissue paper and hangs over edges of table. With kitchen shears, trim edges leaving about 2 in. of dough overhanging on all sides. Allow stretched dough to dry about 5 min., or until it is no longer sticky. Avoid drying dough too long since it will become brittle.
14. Sprinkle butter and bread crumbs, or butter alone, over dough as directed in recipe for filling. Cover dough with the filling.
15. *For Rolling and Baking*—Fold the overhanging dough on all sides over the filling, making Strudel even with edge of table. Beginning at one narrow end of table, grasp the cloth with both hands; slowly lift cloth and fold over a strip of dough about 3 in. wide. Pull cloth toward you; again lift cloth and slowly and loosely roll dough, keeping roll about 3 in. wide. Brush off excess flour from the roll; cut roll into halves and place onto pan. Brush top and sides of Strudel with egg.
16. Bake at 350°F 35 to 45 min., or until Strudel is golden brown. Remove to cooling rack. Sift confectioners' sugar over top of Strudel.
17. Cut Strudel into 2½-in. slices and serve warm or cooled.

12 slices

Note: The perfect strudel is crisp and flaky.

Cherry Filling

2   **16 oz. cans tart red pitted cherries (about 3 cups, drained)**

¾   **cup (about ¼ lb.) almonds**

1¼   **cups sugar (depending on tartness of cherries)**

½   **teaspoon cinnamon**

¼   **cup butter, melted and cooled**

½   **cup (about 1½ slices) fine, dry bread crumbs**

1. Two or three hours before preparing Strudel Dough, set a large sieve over a bowl and empty into it of tart red pitted cherries.
2. Set cherries aside to drain, occasionally shaking sieve to remove as much liquid as possible. (Liquid is not used.)
3. While Strudel Dough is resting 30 min., blanch and toast almonds.
4. Chop almonds and combine with sugar and cinnamon.
5. Set almond mixture aside.
6. Place cherries between layers of absorbent paper and gently pat to remove any excess liquid.
7. After Strudel Dough is stretched and slightly dried, sprinkle butter and bread crumbs over the dough in order listed.
8. Spoon cherries and the almond mixture evenly over the bread crumbs.

Poppy Seed Filling

½   **lb. (about 2½ cups) freshly ground poppy seeds**

1   **cup sugar**

½   **cup (about 2½ oz. raisins**

2   **teaspoons grated lemon peel**

½   **cup butter, melted and cooled**

1. Mix poppy seeds, sugar, raisins and lemon peel together and set aside.
2. After Strudel Dough is stretched and slightly dried, sprinkle butter evenly over it.
3. Spoon poppy seed mixture over the butter.

Apple Filling

4   **medium-size (about 1½ lbs.) cooking apples**

½   **cup butter, melted and cooled**

¼   **cup (about 1 slice) fine, dry bread crumbs**

½   **cup (about 2½ oz.) raisins**

¾   **cup sugar (depending on tartness of apples)**

1   **teaspoon cinnamon**

1. Wash, quarter, core and pare apples.
2. Cut apples into slices 1/8 in. thick and set aside.
3. Sprinkle butter and bread crumbs evenly over the stretched and slightly dried Strudel Dough in order listed.
4. Cover crumbs with the apple slices and raisins.
5. Sprinkle over apples and raisins a mixture of sugar and cinnamon.

Cottage Cheese Filling

2   **egg yolks**
¼   **cup sugar**
¼   **teaspoon salt**
1   **lb. (about 2 cups, firmly packed) dry cottage cheese**
¼   **cup (about 1 oz.) raisins**
½   **teaspoon vanilla extract**
½   **teaspoon grated lemon peel**
½   **cup butter, melted and cooled**
¼   **cup (about 1 slice) fine, dry bread crumbs**

1. Place egg yolks, sugar and salt into a large bowl and beat until thick and lemon colored.
2. Add cottage cheese gradually to egg yolk mixture, blending after each addition.
3. Mix in raisins, vanilla extract and lemon peel.
4. Set cottage cheese mixture aside.
5. After Strudel Dough is stretched and slightly dried, sprinkle butter and bread crumbs over it in order listed.
6. Spoon the cottage cheese mixture in small mounds evenly over dough. Spread mounds carefully with spatula.

Nut Filling

1   **cup (about 4 oz.) walnuts (about 1¾ cups, grated)**
1   **cup (about 4 oz.) coarsely chopped walnuts**
1   **cup (about 5 oz.) raisins**
½   **cup sugar**
3   **tablespoons lemon juice**
2   **teaspoons grated lemon peel**
½   **cup butter, melted and cooled**

1. Grate walnuts.
2. Mix the grated walnuts with 1 cup chopped walnuts, raisins, sugar, lemon juice and lemon peel.
3. Set nut mixture aside.
4. After Strudel Dough is stretched and slightly dried, sprinkle butter evenly over it.
5. Spoon the nut mixture over the butter.

Rice-Fruit Dessert

1   **qt. water**
1½   **teaspoons salt**
½   **cup uncooked rice**
1   **cup sliced strawberries**
1   **cup sliced peaches**
4   **tablespoons sugar (depending upon tartness of fruit)**
1   **cup chilled whipping cream**
¼   **cup Vanilla Confectioners' Sugar (page 60)**

1. Set a 1-qt. bowl and rotary beater in refrigerator to chill.
2. Bring water and salt to boiling in a saucepan.
3. So boiling will not stop, add uncooked rice gradually to water.
4. (The Rice Industry no longer considers it necessary to wash rice before cooking.) Boil rapidly, uncovered, 15 to 20 min., or until a kernel is entirely soft when pressed between fingers. Drain rice in colander or sieve and rinse with hot water to remove loose starch. Cool rice completely.
5. When rice is cool, gently mix together sliced strawberries, peaches and sugar (depending upon tartness of fruit).
6. Using the chilled bowl and beater, beat chilled whipping cream until cream stands in peaks when beater is slowly lifted

upright.

7. Beat vanilla confectioners' sugar in with final few strokes.

8. Fold whipped cream into cooled rice.

9. Arrange alternate layers of rice mixture and fruit in serving bowl, beginning and ending with rice mixture. Chill several hours.

About 6 servings

Love Letters

2	**cups sifted all-purpose flour**
2	**tablespoons sugar**
¼	**teaspoon salt**
¾	**cup butter, chilled and cut in pieces**
4	**egg yolks, slightly beaten**
½	**cup (about 2 oz.) coarsely chopped walnuts**
1	**teaspoon grated lemon peel**
2	**egg whites**
¼	**cup sugar**
½	**teaspoon cinnamon**
	Egg, slightly beaten
3	**tablespoons confectioners' sugar**
1	**teaspoon cinnamon**

1. Lightly grease baking sheets.

2. For Dough—Sift together all-purpose flour, 2 tablespoons sugar and salt into a large bowl.

3. Work butter into dry ingredients by pressing against bottom and sides of bowl with a fork.

4. Add egg yolks gradually to butter-flour mixture, blending ingredients with a fork.

5. (Mixture will be crumbly.) Gather dough into a ball. Turn out onto lightly floured surface. Work with hands, squeezing dough until well blended. Shape into smooth ball with palms of hands. Divide dough into halves; wrap in waxed paper and place in refrigerator for about 1 hr. Shape dough in a very cool kitchen.

6. After 45 min., prepare filling.

7. For Filling—Mix together chopped walnuts and grated lemon peel.

8. Set aside.

9. Beat egg whites until frothy.

10. Add ¼ cup sugar and ½ teaspoons cinnamon gradually to egg whites, beating well after each addition.

11. Beat until very stiff peaks are formed. Gently fold nut mixture into the egg whites.

12. Set filling aside.

13. To Form Love Letters—Remove one-half of dough from refrigerator. Place dough on lightly floured surface and roll into rectangle 1/16 in. thick. Work quickly to prevent dough from becoming too soft. With knife or spatula, gently loosen dough from board wherever sticking occurs; lift dough slightly and sprinkle flour underneath. Trim off uneven edges of rectangle. Gather trimmings into a ball; wrap in waxed paper and place into refrigerator.

14. Cut rectangle into 3-in. squares. Place about 2 teaspoons of the filling onto center of each square. To make "letters," bring opposite corners together, overlapping slightly at center. Repeat with other two corners. Place on baking sheet. In this way, continue to make Love Letters and place 1 in. apart on baking sheet. Brush Love Letters with egg, slightly beaten.

15. Bake at 350°F 20 to 30 min., or until lightly browned. Carefully remove Love Letters from baking sheets to cooling racks. When cooled, sift over them a mixture of confectioners' sugar and cinnamon.

About 2½ doz. Love Letters

Apricot Ice Cream 76

Suet Pastry

½ lb. beef suet
1 cup sifted all-purpose flour
½ teaspoon salt
2 cups sifted all-purpose flour
¼ cup milk
1 pkg. active dry yeast
¼ cup warm water (110°F to 115°F. If using compressed yeast, soften 1 cake in ¼ cup lukewarm water, 80°F to 85°F.)
1 tablespoon sugar
½ teaspoon salt
1 egg yolk
1 tablespoon lemon juice
   Egg, slightly beaten

1. Set out 2 shallow baking sheets, having 4 sides; do not grease.
2. Have beef suet ready.
3. Break suet into small pieces, removing and discarding the membrane which coats it.
4. Sift together all-purpose flour and salt onto pastry board.
5. Press suet into flour with heel of hand until well blended. Shape suet mixture into a rectangle 2 in. thick; wrap in waxed paper and set aside in refrigerator.
6. Measure 1¾ to 2 cups all-purpose flour and set aside.
7. Scald milk.
8. Meanwhile, soften dry yeast in warm water.
9. Set aside.
10. Put sugar and salt into a bowl.
11. Immediately pour the scalded milk over ingredients in bowl. When mixture is lukewarm, blend in ¼ cup of the sifted flour, beating until smooth. Stir the softened yeast and add, mixing well. Add about one-half of the remaining flour to the dough and beat until very smooth. Beat in egg yolk and lemon juice.
12. Then beat in enough of the remaining flour to make a soft dough. Turn dough onto a lightly floured surface and let stand 5 to 10 min. Knead dough. Cover dough with inverted bowl and let rest about 15 min. in warm place.
13. Lightly flour rolling pin. Roll dough on a lightly floured surface into a rectangle ½ in. thick around edges, leaving center slightly thicker.
14. Keep corners square, gently pulling dough into shape where necessary. With knife or spatula, loosen pastry from surface wherever sticking occurs; lift pastry slightly and sprinkle flour underneath.
15. Remove suet mixture from refrigerator; place on center of rolled dough. Fold edges of dough over suet mixture. Turn the dough upside down. Flatten with rolling pin, pressing down heavily while rolling. Make a rectangle about 14 in. long and 24 in. wide. Fold right third of dough over middle section. Fold left third over the right third. Let dough rest 5 min. Turn dough one quarter way around to have overlapping open edge away from you. Turn dough upside down. Again roll dough into rectangle about 14 in. long and 24 in. wide. Repeat folding, resting, turning one quarter way around and turning dough upside down. Follow directions for shaping dough into Crescents, Squares or Biscuits. Place pastries onto baking sheets. Brush each pastry with egg, slightly beaten.
16. Set pastry aside 15 min.; brush again with some of remaining egg.
17. Bake at 350°F 20 to 30 min., or until golden brown.

About 3 doz. crescents or squares;
about 2 doz. biscuits

Suet Pastry Crescents:
Follow recipe for Suet Pastry. After second folding process. roll dough into 3-in. squares. Set out ⅔ cup thick **jam** such as apricot or strawberry. Spoon about ¾ teaspoon jam diagonally across center of each square. Starting at one of the corners. roll each square and turn ends slightly toward middle to form crescents. Press ends slightly with fingers to completely seal in jam. Place crescents, with overlapping edges underneath, about 1-in. apart onto baking sheets.

Suet Pastry Squares:
Follow recipe for Suet Pastry Crescents but place jam at center of each square. Bring four corners of the square up toward center, pressing points together slightly with fingers to seal at the mid-point. Place squares about 1 in. apart onto baking sheets.

Suet Pastry Biscuits:
Follow recipe for Suet Pastry. After second folding process, roll dough into a rectangle ½-in. thick. Score top of biscuit dough with sharp long-bladed knife by starting at upper left corner of rectangle and making diagonal cuts 1/8 in. deep and ¼ in. apart across dough. Repeat, starting at upper right corner. Cut biscuits with a lightly floured 2-in. biscuit cutter using an even pressure to keep sides of biscuits straight. Place biscuits about 1 in. apart onto baking sheets. Gather remaining dough by pushing pieces together without stacking. Avoid over-handling dough. Make top smooth with rolling pin. Make diagonal cuts across top of dough as before and cut out additional biscuits. Place onto baking sheets.

Note: Caraway seeds may be sprinkled onto top of biscuits just before baking.

Ischl Cookies

½	cup (about 3 oz.) hazelnuts (about 1 cup, grated)
1½	cups sifted all-purpose flour
¼	teaspoon cinnamon
¼	teaspoon cocoa
¾	cup unsalted butter
1	teaspoon grated lemon peel
½	teaspoon lemon juice
¾	cup confectioners' sugar
¼	cup thick jam, such as apricot or strawberry
¼	cup whole blanched almonds
¾	lb. semi-sweet candymaking chocolate

1. Lightly grease cookie sheets.
2. Grate hazelnuts and set aside.
3. Sift together all-purpose flour, cinnamon and cocoa and set aside.
4. Cream unsalted butter, grated lemon peel and lemon juice until butter is softened.
5. Add confectioners' sugar gradually, creaming until fluffy after each addition.
6. Blend in the ground nuts.
7. Add the dry ingredients to creamed mixture in fourths, mixing until blended after each addition. Cover bowl with waxed paper and let dough rest 15 min. Roll dough on lightly floured surface to ¼-in. thickness. Cut into rounds with a lightly floured 1½-in. cookie cutter. Place rounds about 1 in. apart onto cookie sheets.
8. Bake at 350°F 15 to 20 min., or until lightly browned; remove cookies to cooling racks.
9. While cookies are cooling, set out jam and blanched almonds.
10. When cookies are cool, turn one-half of the cookies upside down and spread about ½ teaspoon jam on each. Make cookies sandwiches by placing remaining cookies on top of jam; set aside. Set almonds aside to be used as a garnish for the cookies.
11. Set out two cooling racks, each over a piece of waxed paper.
12. Partially melt semi-sweet candymaking chocolate over simmering water, being careful not to overheat.
13. Remove chocolate from the simmering water and stir until completely melted. Dip top of sandwich cookies into chocolate. Place cookies, chocolate-side up, onto one of the cooling racks; let excess chocolate drip off cookies onto the waxed paper. (Scrape together and wrap excess chocolate; store for future use.) Immediately top each cookie with one of the reserved almonds; cool cookies until chocolate coating is firm. Refrigerate if necessary.

About 2 doz. cookies

Apple-Filled Pastry

5	cups sifted all-purpose flour
¼	cup sugar
1½	teaspoons salt
1¼	cups butter, chilled and cut in pieces
4	egg yolks, slightly beaten
½	cup thick sour cream
¼	cup (about 1 slice) fine, dry bread crumbs
4	medium-size (about 1½ lbs.) cooking apples (4½ to 5 cups, sliced)
1	tablespoon lemon juice
2	teaspoons grated lemon peel
½	cup (about 2½ oz.) raisins
½	cup sugar (depending upon tartness of apples)
1½	teaspoons cinnamon
3	egg whites
6	tablespoons sugar
	Egg, slightly beaten
3	tablespoons confectioners' sugar

1. For Pastry—Set out a 15½x10½x1-in. jelly roll pan.

2. Sift together all-purpose flour, ¼ cup sugar and salt into a large bowl.

3. Work butter into dry ingredients, by pressing against bottom and sides of bowl with a fork.

4. Add egg yolks and sour cream gradually to the ingredients in the bowl, mixing with a fork after each addition.

5. (Mixture will be crumbly.) Gather dough into a ball. Turn out onto lightly floured surface. Work with hands, squeezing dough until well blended. Shape into a smooth roll with palms of hands. Cut off one third of dough for top pastry; wrap in waxed paper and place it into refrigerator. Roll remaining dough into a rectangle to fit bottom of pan. Place into pan; with a fork, prick dough at 1-in. intervals.

6. Bake at 450°F 10 min. Remove pan from oven to cooling rack; reduce oven heat to 350°F. Sprinkle dry bread crumbs evenly over the baked pastry.

7. Set aside.

8. For Filling—Wash, quarter, core, pare and thinly slice apples into a bowl.

9. Immediately toss apples with a mixture of lemon juice, grated lemon peel and lightly mix with a mixture of raisins, ⅓ to ½ cup sugar (depending upon tartness of apples) and cinnamon.

10. Set apple mixture aside.

11. Beat egg whites until frothy.

12. Add sugar gradually to egg whites, beating well after each addition.

13. Continue beating until very stiff peaks are formed. Gently place beaten egg whites onto apple mixture and fold. Set the filling aside.

14. For Completing Pastry—Remove remaining pastry from refrigerator and roll into a rectangle ½ in. larger than the pan. With fork, prick top pastry at 2-in. intervals. With spatula loosen pastry.

15. Spoon apple filling evenly over the bread crumbs on bottom pastry.

16. Fold top pastry in half; lift gently and place onto apple mixture; unfold. Gently press edges of top pastry against sides of pan to seal. Brush top of pastry with egg.

17. Bake at 350°F 25 to 30 min., or until pastry is golden brown and apples are tender when pierced with a fork. Remove pan from oven; set onto cooling rack and cut pastry into 2½-in. squares. Sprinkle confectioners' sugar onto the pastry squares.

18. Serve warm or cold.

2 doz. squares

Apple-Filled Pastry with Nuts: Follow recipe for Apple-Filled Pastry. Substitute 1 cup (about 4 oz.) coarsely chopped **walnuts** for raisins.

Nut-Filled Crescents

2	cups (about ½ lb.) walnuts, ground
½	cup sugar
3	egg whites, slightly beaten
2	tablespoons milk
3	cups sifted all-purpose flour
1	cup unsalted butter, chilled and cut in pieces
3	egg yolks, slightly beaten
1½	tablespoons cream
2	teaspoons grated lemon peel
	Confectioners' sugar
	Egg, slightly beaten
2	tablespoons Vanilla Confectioners' Sugar (page 60)

1. Lightly grease cookie sheets.
2. For Nut Filling—Mix walnuts, sugar, egg whites and milk thoroughly and set aside.
3. For Dough—Place all-purpose flour into a large bowl.
4. Work unsalted butter into flour by pressing against bottom and sides of bowl with a fork.
5. Add a mixture of egg yolks, cream and grated lemon peel gradually to ingredients in the bowl, mixing thoroughly with a fork.
6. (Mixture will be crumbly.) Gather dough into a ball. Turn out onto lightly floured surface. Work with hands, squeezing dough until well blended. With palms of hands shape dough into smooth roll. Slice into 48 pieces. (If dough is too soft and sticky to handle, chill for a short time.) Shape pieces into balls.
7. For Crescents—Lightly sprinkle a small area of working surface with confectioners' sugar.
8. Roll one ball at a time into a circle about 1/16 in. thick. Spread dough with 2 teaspoons of the filling. Gently lifting nearest edge, roll; shape into crescent by curving ends of roll slightly. Place crescent onto cookie sheet with overlapping edge underneath. In this way, make other crescents, lightly sprinkling confectioners' sugar onto working surface each time. Brush crescents with egg.
9. Bake at 375°F 15 to 20 min., or until lightly browned; remove to cooling racks.
10. Just before serving crescents, sprinkle with vanilla confectioners' sugar.
11. Shake off excess sugar.

4 doz. crescents

Poppy Seed Crescents: Follow recipe for Nut-Filled Crescents. Substitute **Poppy Seed Filling** for Nut Filling. For Poppy Seed Filling—Combine in a heavy 1½ qt. saucepan 3 cups (about ⅔ lb.) freshly ground **poppy seeds**, 1¼ cups **sugar**, ¾ cup **milk** and ½ cup **butter.** Cook over low heat, stirring constantly, about 5 min., or until mixture is slightly thickened. Remove from heat and cool. (If, on standing, filling becomes too thick to spread easily, stir in a small amount of milk.)

Almond Sticks

¾	cup (about ¼ lb.) almonds (about 2 cups, grated)
½	cup unsalted butter
1	cup sifted confectioners' sugar
1	cup sifted all-purpose flour
½	cup Vanilla Confectioners' Sugar (page 60)

1. Lightly grease cookie sheets.
2. Grate almonds and set aside.
3. Put unsalted butter into bowl and cream until softened.
4. Add confectioners' sugar to the butter, creaming until fluffy after each addition.
5. Add to the butter mixture, stirring just until the ingredients are blended, a mixture of the almonds and all-purpose flour.
6. Gather dough into a ball. Turn dough out onto lightly floured surface and roll into a rectangle ½ in. thick, keeping edges straight. Cut dough into strips 2½x½-in. and place strips 1 in. apart onto cookie sheets.
7. Bake at 350°F 20 to 25 min., or until cookies are lightly browned. Immediately remove to cooling racks. When cooled, roll in vanilla confectioners' sugar.

About 3 doz. cookies

Hazelnut Sticks: Follow recipe for Almond Sticks. Substitute 1 cup plus 2 tablespoons (about 5 oz.) **hazelnuts** (about 2 cups, grated) for almonds.

Linzer Wreath Cookies

¼	cup (about 1 oz.) finely chopped walnuts
¼	cup sugar
2	cups sifted all-purpose flour
½	cup confectioners' sugar
¼	teaspoon baking soda
½	cup unsalted butter, chilled and cut in pieces
2	egg yolks, slightly beaten
¼	teaspoon vanilla extract
¼	teaspoon grated lemon peel
	Egg, slightly beaten
¼	cup thick jam, such as apricot or strawberry
2	tablespoons confectioners' sugar

1. Lightly grease cookie sheets.
2. Mix together walnuts and sugar and set aside.
3. Sift together all-purpose flour, confectioners' sugar and baking soda.
4. Work unsalted butter into the dry ingredients by pressing against bottom and sides of bowl with a fork.
5. Gradually add to the ingredients in the bowl, mixing with a fork after each addition, a mixture of egg yolks, vanilla extract and grated lemon peel.
6. (Mixture will be crumbly.) Gather dough into a ball. Turn dough out onto lightly floured surface. Work with hands, squeezing dough until well blended. Shape into smooth ball with palms of hands. If dough becomes too soft chill slightly in refrigerator.
7. Roll dough 1/8 to ¼ in. thick. With lightly floured 2-in. scallop-edged cookie cutter, cut dough into rounds. Place one-half of the rounds onto cookie sheets. Using a thimble dipped in flour, cut ½-in. holes in centers of remaining rounds, forming rings. Brush all the rounds and rings with egg.
8. Dip top surface of rings into the nut-sugar mixture.
9. Place rings, coated-side up, on cookie sheets (not on top of cookie rounds).
10. Bake at 350°F 15 to 20 min., or until lightly browned. Remove cookie to cooling racks.
11. Set out jam, such as apricot or strawberry.
12. Spread ½ to ¾ teaspoon of the jam onto each plain cookie round. Top each with a nut-topped cookie ring. Sprinkle confectioners' sugar onto cookies.

About 1½ doz. cookies

Deep-Fried Cookies

Hydrogenated vegetable
shortening, all-purpose
shortening, lard or cook-
ing oil for deep-frying
2　cups sifted all-purpose
　　flour
1　tablespoon sugar
½　teaspoon salt
3　egg yolks, slightly beaten
½　cup thick sour cream
½　teaspoon vanilla extract
3　tablespoons confectioners'
　　sugar (or Vanilla Confec-
　　tioners' Sugar, page 60)

1. About 20 min. before deep-frying, fill a deep saucepan one-half to two-thirds full with shortening for deep-frying.
2. Heat slowly to 365°F. When using an automatic deep-fryer, follow manufacturer's directions for amount of fat and timing.
3. Meanwhile, sift together all-purpose flour, sugar and salt into a bowl.
4. Make a well in center of dry ingredients and pour in mixture of egg yolks, sour cream and vanilla extract.
5. Blend ingredients until all the flour is moistened. Let dough rest 1 or 2 min. Turn dough out onto lightly floured surface and knead, only until ingredients are well blended. Shape dough into a smooth ball; roll dough on lightly floured surface into a rectangle 1/8 in. thick. (If space will not permit, roll only one-half of dough at a time.) With spatula, loosen dough from board wherever sticking occurs; lift dough slightly and sprinkle a little flour underneath. With floured knife cut dough into diamond-shape pieces 2 in. wide at center and 6 in. long. (A cardboard pattern may be used.) Make a 1-in. lengthwise cut in the center of each diamond; pull one end through slit, twisting slightly.
6. Deep-fry only one layer of cookies at one time; do not crowd. Turn cookies with fork as they rise to surface and several times during cooking, but do not pierce. Fry about 3 min., or until lightly browned. Drain cookies over fat for a second before removing to absorbent paper. Sprinkle cookies with confectioners' sugar (or Vanilla Confectioners' Sugar, page 60).

About 2½ doz. cookies

Golden Coffee Cake

5 cups sifted all-purpose flour
½ cup milk
2 pkgs. active dry yeast
½ cup warm water (110°F to 115°F. If compressed yeast is used, soften 2 cakes in ½ cup lukewarm water, 80°F to 85°F.)
½ cup shortening
½ cup sugar
1½ teaspoon salt
2 eggs, well beaten
1 cup sugar
¾ cup (about 3 oz.) finely chopped walnuts
1½ teaspoons cinnamon
½ cup butter, melted
½ cup (about 2½ oz.) raisins

1. A 10-in. tubed pan will be needed.
2. Measure all-purpose flour and set aside.
3. Scald milk.
4. Meanwhile, soften dry yeast in warm water.
5. Set aside.
6. Put shortening, sugar and salt into a large bowl.
7. Immediately pour the scalded milk over ingredients in bowl. When mixture is lukewarm, mix in ½ cup of the sifted flour, beating until dough is smooth. Stir the softened yeast and add to dough, mixing well. Add about one-half of the remaining flour and beat until very smooth. Beat in eggs.
8. Then beat in enough of remaining flour to make a soft dough. Turn dough onto a lightly floured surface and let it rest 5 to 10 min. Knead.
9. Form dough into a large ball and put into a greased bowl. Turn dough over to bring greased surface to top. Cover bowl with waxed paper and towel and let stand in warm place (about 80°F) until dough is doubled. Punch dough down with fist; pull edges in to center and completely turn dough over in bowl. Cover bowl and let dough rise again until nearly doubled.
10. Meanwhile, lightly grease the bottom of the tubed pan.
11. Mix together sugar, walnuts and cinnamon in a shallow dish and set aside.
12. Place melted butter into another shallow dish and set aside.
13. Measure raisins and set aside.
14. Tear off bits of dough and form into balls about 1¼ in. in diameter. Roll balls first into butter then roll lightly in sugar mixture. Arrange layer of balls in the tubed pan so that they do not touch each other. Sprinkle about one-third of the raisins over balls and slightly press raisins into balls. Continue in this manner until all dough is made into balls and arranged in the pan and all raisins are used. Sprinkle any remaining sugar mixture or butter over top layer of balls. Cover pan with waxed paper and towel and let dough rise again 30 to 45 min., or until light.
15. Bake at 375°F 35 to 40 min., or until golden brown. Run spatula around sides of coffee cake. Invert onto plate. To serve, break coffee cake apart with two forks.

8 to 10 servings

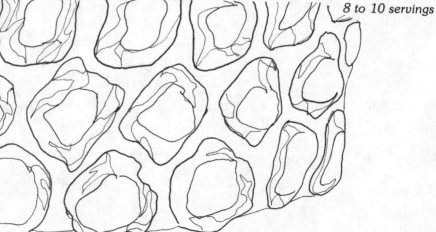

Almond Coffee Cake Braid

4½ cups sifted all-purpose flour
¾ cup milk
1 pkg. active dry yeast
¼ cup warm water (110°F to 115°F. If using compressed yeast, soften 1 cake in ¼ cup lukewarm water, 80°F to 85°F.)
⅓ cup sugar
⅓ cup butter
1½ teaspoons salt
1 egg, well beaten
½ cup (about 2½ oz.) raisins
½ cup (about 3 oz.) almonds, blanched, toasted and coarsely chopped
2 teaspoons grated lemon peel
1 teaspoon lemon juice
Egg, slightly beaten

1. A baking sheet will be needed.
2. Measure all-purpose flour and set aside.
3. Scald milk.
4. Meanwhile, soften dry yeast in warm water.
5. Set aside.
6. Put sugar, butter and salt into a large bowl.
7. Immediately pour the scalded milk over ingredients in bowl. When the milk mixture is lukewarm, stir and add ½ cup of the sifted flour, beating until dough is smooth. Stir the softened yeast and add to dough, mixing well. Add about one-half of the remaining flour and beat until very smooth.
8. Beat in egg, raisins, almonds, grated lemon peel and lemon juice.
9. Then beat in enough of remaining flour to make a soft dough. Turn dough onto a lightly floured surface and let stand 5 to 10 min. Knead.
10. Form dough into a large ball and put it into a greased bowl. Turn dough to bring greased surface to top. Cover bowl with waxed paper and towel and let stand in warm place (about 80°F) until dough is doubled. Punch dough down with fist; pull edges of dough in to center and turn dough completely over in bowl. Cover; let dough rise again until nearly doubled.
11. Turn out onto floured surface. Divide dough into halves. Roll each half with palms of hands into a strip 1 in. in diameter and about 26 in. long. To braid, lay one strip horizontally on center of board. Lay other strip vertically on top, crossing at center of first strip. Grasp ends horizontal strip and reverse positions. Do the same with vertical strip. Repeat until all dough is braided.
12. Lightly grease the baking sheet.
13. Place braided dough flat on baking sheet, tucking the ends under the braid. Brush with egg.
14. Let rise again 30 to 45 min., or until light. Brush again with some of the beaten egg.
15. Bake at 350°F 45 to 50 min., or until golden brown. Remove coffee cake to cooling rack. When cool, cut into ½-in. slices.

About 24 slices

Raised Doughnuts

4½ cups sifted all-purpose flour
⅔ cup milk
1 pkg. active dry yeast
¼ cup warm water (110 °F to 115 °F. If using compressed yeast, soften 1 cake in ¼ cup lukewarm water 80 °F to 85 °F.)
½ cup sifted confectioners' sugar
¼ cup butter
¼ teaspoon salt
6 egg yolks, well beaten
1 teaspoon rum
Hydrogenated vegetable shortening, all-purpose shortening, lard or cooking oil for deep-fying
3 tablespoons confectioners' sugar (or Vanilla Confectioners' Sugar, page 60)

1. Measure all-purpose flour and set aside.
2. Scald milk.
3. Meanwhile, soften dry yeast in warm water.
4. Set aside.
5. Put confectioners' sugar, butter and salt into a large bowl.
6. Immediately pour the scalded milk over ingredients in bowl. When the mixture is lukewarm. mix well and stir in about ½ cup of the sifted flour, beating until dough is smooth. Stir the softened yeast and add to dough, mixing well. Add about one-half the remaining flour to the dough and beat until very smooth. Add in thirds, beating well after each addition, a mixture of egg yolks and rum.
7. Then beat in enough of the remaining flour to make a soft dough. Turn dough onto a lightly floured surface and let it rest 5 to 10 min. Knead.
8. Form dough into a large ball and put it into a greased bowl. Turn to bring greased surface to top. Cover bowl with waxed paper and towel and let stand in warm place (about 80 °F) until dough is doubled. Punch dough down with fist; pull edges in to center and turn dough completely over in bowl. Cover bowl and let dough rise again until nearly doubled.
9. Turn dough out on floured surface and roll about 3/8 in. thick. With spatula, loosen dough from board wherever sticking occurs; lightly sprinkle flour underneath. Cut dough into rounds with a 3-in. lightly floured doughnut cutter (no hole in center). Let dough rise again 15 to 25 min., or until light.
10. About 20 min. before deep-frying, fill a deep saucepan one-half to two-thirds full with shortening for deep-frying.
11. Heat slowly to 365 °F. When using automatic deep-fryer, follow manufacturer's directions for amount of fat and timing.
12. Deep-fry the doughnuts 2 or 3 min. or until lightly browned. Deep-fry only one layer of doughnuts at a time; do not crowd. Turn doughnuts occasionally with a fork to brown evenly, but do not pierce. Drain doughnuts over fat for a second before removing to absorbent paper; cool slightly. Sift confectioners' sugar (or vanilla confectioners' sugar over doughnuts.

About 1½ doz. doughnuts

Jam-Filled Doughnuts: Follow recipe for Raised Doughnuts. Make a short slit in side of each cooled doughnut through to the center. Force ½ to 1 teaspoon **jam** or **jelly** into center of each doughnut and close tightly. A pastry bag and decorating tube may be used to force jelly into slit.

Apricot Coffee Cake

3⅓ cups sifted all-purpose
  flour
⅓ cup milk
1 pkg. active dry yeast
¼ cup warm water (110°F to
  115°F. If using compressed
  yeast, soften 1 cake in ¼
  cup lukewarm water, 80°F
  to 85°F.)
¾ cup butter, softened
1 tablespoon sugar
¼ teaspoon salt
2 egg yolks, well beaten
½ cup thick apricot jam

1. An 8-in. sq. cake pan will be needed.
2. Measure all-purpose flour and set aside.
3. Scald milk.
4. Meanwhile, soften dry yeast in warm water.
5. Set aside.
6. Put butter, sugar and salt into a bowl.
7. Immediately pour the scalded milk over ingredients in bowl and stir until butter is melted. When the milk mixture is lukewarm, blend in ⅓ cup of the sifted flour, beating until dough is smooth. Stir the softened yeast and add to dough, mixing well. Add about one-half of the remaining flour to the dough and beat until very smooth. Blend in egg yolks.
8. Then beat in enough of the remaining flour to make a soft dough. Turn dough onto a lightly floured surface and let stand 5 to 10 min. Knead.
9. Form dough into a large ball and place into greased bowl. Turn dough to bring greased surface to top. Cover bowl with waxed paper and towel and let stand in warm place (about 80°F) until dough is doubled. Punch dough down with fist; pull edges of dough in to center and turn dough completely over in bowl. Cover and let rise again until nearly doubled.
10. Meanwhile, grease bottom of the cake pan.
11. Set out apricot jam.
12. Roll dough ¼ in. thick. Cut dough into 2½x4-in. rectangles. Spoon 1 teaspoon of the jam onto the center of each rectangle. Fold each rectangle into lengthwise halves, pinching the two narrow ends together and leaving center open. Stand pieces open-side up and side-by-side in the cake pan. Cover pan with towel. Let dough rise again 15 to 25 min., or until light.
13. Bake at 425°F 15 to 20 min., or until golden brown. Break pieces of coffee cake apart with a fork. Serve warm or cooled.

About 14 pieces

Apricot Ice Cream

1 cup light cream
4 egg yolks
  grated rind from ½
    lemon
3 oz. sugar
6 oz. dried and soaked
    apricots, diced
1 teaspoon gelatin
½ teaspoon vanilla
6 dried, finely chopped
    apricots
1 cup heavy cream, whipped

1. Beat the egg yolks in the cream in a heavy saucepan. Add grated lemon rind and sugar and whip the cream continuously while heating slowly. Remove from heat when cream starts to simmer, but go on whipping while it cools down.
2. Mix gelatin with 2 tablespoons hot water
3. Add gelatin and vanilla to diced apricots. Chill until about to set.
4. Fold cream into gelatin mixture.
5. Freeze the cream for at least 3 hours and whip it a few times during that time. The apricot ice cream is spooned up in tall glasses and decorated with finely chopped dried apricots and whipped cream.

6 servings.

HUNGARIAN INDEX

Index